BIBLE STORIES
In Colour

BIBLE STORIES
In Colour

by
Rev. Dr. J. F. Allen

illustrated by
Alvaro Mairani

HAMLYN

LONDON   NEW YORK   SYDNEY   TORONTO

Published 1975
The Hamlyn Publishing Group Limited
London. New York. Sydney. Toronto
Astronaut House. Feltham. Middlesex
© Pioneer Publishing Company
© Text copyright this edition 1975
The Hamlyn Publishing Group Limited
Printed in Spain
ISBN 0 600 313 557
Printed and bound by Novograph, S. A.
and Roner, S. A.
Crta. de Irun Km. 12,500-Madrid
D.L.: M-1109-1975.

BIBLE STORIES
In Colour

CONTENTS

NOAH AND THE ARK

As the years went by, the earth, which had been a pleasant place to live in, began to show signs of restlessness. People became more wicked. They started to hate and kill. They thought only of pleasure and themselves. They lied, cheated, became drunk, and even stole from their neighbours.

There were some people left on earth, who in spite of all the wickedness around them, remained good, but they were so few, that there was nothing they could do to put the world right again.

When God saw that there was no hope for the wretched people who carried on in their evil ways, He decided to destroy everything that He had made – they were not fit to walk on the face of the earth, and God was sorry that He had ever made it.

Now, there was at this time, a man called Noah, who refused to fall into bad ways. He did his best to look after his family, and protect them from the wrong-doers. Noah was very hardworking and loyal to God, whom he always tried to please. He was by trade a carpenter, and a builder, and his three sons, Shem, Ham and Japheth worked with him, making carts and building houses. They were not lazy and wicked;

neither were their wives. Their only thought was to do good, and live a good life.

When God saw this, He knew in his heart that He must save Noah and his family, because they did not deserve to die, so when God was ready, He called to Noah saying:

"This is the end. The earth is filled with violence, and the time has come for Me to destroy it and all the people – none shall be saved, except you, Noah, and your family." Then God said:

"I want you to build yourself a great ark. You must use gopher wood, and cover the ark with pitch. Inside you must build many rooms, and take with you into it your wife and three sons, and their wives. Also each kind of animal, bird and creeping thing, take one pair; but of the animals which men use most, like sheep, goats, and cattle, and the birds of the air, you must take seven pairs of each kind. Of them you must be sure that you take male and female, so that their kind may be kept alive on earth."

God gave Noah the exact measurements that he should use when building the ark, and when all this was explained He said: "Behold! I will bring a great flood upon the earth, and everything in it will surely die."

And so Noah began building the ark, but first he made a plan, as God had instructed him to do. When the people who lived nearby saw Noah and his sons building the ark, which looked something like a boat,

they thought the family had gone mad. They just couldn't understand why Noah needed to build such a thing, when there was no sea around them on which to float it, when it was ready.

"What use will it be?" they said amongst themselves, and many of them laughed together as the ark began to take shape.

It took a long time to finish, but Noah and his sons took no notice of their neighbours as they gathered to stare at the vessel, which was being built in a field near Noah's house.

Noah knew he had to obey God's word or he and his family would perish when the floods came, as God had said they would.

Apart from building the ark, Noah and his sons spent hours hunting the animals God had asked them to find. Cages had to be built and the animals fed.

At last the ark was finished. It stood three storeys high and had windows and a door, and had been made watertight with pitch. Noah and his sons had stored enormous quantities of food for themselves, and the animals, and when all was ready God told Noah to take his family inside the ark, and then lead in all the creatures two by two, male and female.

When they were all safely inside, God closed the door of the ark Himself, and for seven days they waited.

Then as God had said, the floods began. The rains poured down in fury, and as the houses and trees were

covered up there was nowhere on earth for the people or the animals to go, and they all perished.

Still the floods came, and even the highest mountain peaks disappeared and it was impossible to tell the difference between land and sea. For forty days and forty nights the storms raged, but as the waters rose, the ark was safe, as God had promised.

Inside the ark Noah and his family were not afraid because they knew God was with them, and after another hundred and fifty days God stopped the rains.

As the waters went down, the ark was stranded on top of Mount Ararat. Noah sent a raven and a dove to see whether the waters had dried up. The dove could not find anywhere to settle, because the earth was still covered with water, and Noah took her back into the ark.

Seven days later he sent the dove out again, but it was not until evening that she returned with an olive leaf in her beak, and Noah knew that the trees were appearing, and the land was almost dry.

When he sent the dove out again she did not return, and Noah knew it was safe for him to open the door of the ark.

Then God told Noah to take his family and all the animals and birds and let them all multiply because he would never destroy the earth again.

After he had fetched his family and let the animals go, Noah went to a quiet place to build an altar to God, and worship Him there.

God spoke again to Noah and said: "While the earth remains, seed time and harvest, cold and heat, summer and winter, day and night shall not cease." God blessed Noah, and said he would put a rainbow in the clouds as a reminder of his everlasting promise not to destroy the earth, and all that is within it.

Then Noah rose up and went out with his family to build a new world.

ABRAHAM AND ISAAC

Abram and his wife Sarai lived in Canaan at Bethel. They had gone there from the country of Chaldees far to the east, because God had asked Abram to go there.

When they first reached Canaan there was a terrible famine and they went further south to Egypt. But when the rains came and there was food again and pasture for their cattle, they returned to Bethel.

Abram, and his nephew, Lot, became rich, with much gold and silver, and large herds of cattle and sheep, but their herdsmen quarrelled because there was not enough grazing, and Abram and Lot decided to split their herds.

Although Abram was an old man, he was good and kind-hearted, and gave Lot first choice of land. Lot chose the rich-looking parts near the river Jordan, and Abram was left with the poorer areas near Bethel.

But God said he would help Abram, and told him that all the land as far as he could see would become his, and his descendants would multiply.

Abram moved his herds to Mamre near Hebron, but as he was ninety-nine, and his wife Sarai was ninety, and they had no children, Abram could not understand how they could have many descendants as God had promised.

Then God told Abram again that he would be blessed with many descendants, and would become the father of many nations. "Your name is now Abraham which means 'the Father of a multitude,' God told him. "And Sarai will be known as Sarah, which means 'Princess', and she will have a son, and I will bless her, and make her the mother of nations, and Canaan will be your land."

But when Abraham heard that, he threw himself down on his face, and couldn't help laughing in his heart. How could this possibly happen, with both of them so old? But God knew what he was thinking, and said: "You have laughed, but I have said it, and a son will be born to you. And because of your laughter, that son will be called Isaac. He will share in the promise I have made to you, and become the father of many nations."

Still no baby came, though. Abraham and Sarah must have wondered what was happening. Then one very hot day when Abraham was sitting in his tent doorway at Mamre, he saw coming towards him three men. As great a man as he was, he ran to them, and bowed himself to the ground in front of them, and begged them to come in and rest a while. He knew these were no ordinary men! He brought water to wash their feet, and sent his servants quickly to get bread and meat ready for them. When they ate, Abraham himself stood next to them as their servant. The visitors asked him where his wife, Sarah was.

When he told them that she was in the tent, One of them said: "I shall come back to you in the spring-time, and Sarah will have a son."

Now Sarah was listening to all they said; and in her heart she laughed when she heard again about the baby. But the Man who had spoken, said to Abraham: "Why did Sarah laugh, not believing that she could have a baby? I tell you again that I will return to you in the spring-time, and Sarah will have a son." Then Sarah spoke up and said that she hadn't laughed. But God – because it was God Who had come to them – said: "Don't deny it! You did laugh."

Soon afterwards the three visitors left the camp again, and went off into the desert.

In the spring-time, as God had promised, Sarah had a son, and Abraham called him Isaac, just as he had been told to do.

What a great feast was held, because of the wonderful gift from God to Abraham and Sarah in their old age! Joy had come to their hearts at last. God had kept His promise to them, and now they could believe that He would give them descendants, like the dust of the earth in number, just as He had said.

Some years later, when Isaac was a boy in his teens, God put his father, Abraham, to the test. He gave him an awful commandment. "Abraham," He said, "take your son, your only son, the one you love so much, away into the land of Moriah, and offer him there to Me as a burnt-offering." How terrible Abraham must

have felt. That meant he must kill his own son, and offer him to God. What would happen to all the promises of many descendants now?

But Abraham trusted God, and obeyed the commandment. Early the next morning he got up and prepared for the long journey to the land of Moriah. He called two servants to saddle his ass, and fasten on its back enough split wood for the fire on which he had to make the sacrifice. Then with Isaac the party moved off.

On the third day Abraham saw the place where the sacrifice was to be made. Isaac carried the wood, and Abraham carried the fire and a knife, but when Isaac asked him where the lamb was for the burnt offering, Abraham only answered that God would provide the lamb.

They made an altar of stones and laid on it the wood. Then Abraham bound Isaac, and put him on the altar, but as he raised the knife the Angel of God called and told him that because Abraham was willing to obey God's commandment and trusted God with all his heart, his son would be saved.

Then Abraham saw a ram caught by its horns in a bush and offered it as a burnt offering to God, who again told him that he would increase his descendants.

Abraham moved his camp to Beersheba where there was grazing for the cattle, and there Sarah died when she was a hundred and twenty seven years old.

Abraham was worried that Isaac had not married,

but he did not want him to marry a woman of Canaan, and sent a servant to Nahor to find a wife.

The servant saw the women of Nahor going to fetch water, and prayed that God would direct him to ask the right girl for a drink of water from her pitcher.

It was Rebekah, the daughter of Bethuel, Abraham's nephew who gave him water and who eventually accompanied him back to Beersheba.

One day, as the sun was setting, Isaac saw the servant's camel train, bringing the girl who was to become his wife.

And when Rebekah saw Isaac she too fell in love with him. They were married and Rebekah became a great comfort to Isaac and they were a joy to Abraham until he died at the age of one hundred and seventy-five years.

JACOB AND ESAU

Isaac and Rebekah lived in the land of Canaan, and had twin sons called Esau and Jacob.

Esau was a little older than Jacob and had red hair over most of his body. Jacob was different and had a smooth skin.

Now Esau grew to love hunting, while Jacob preferred farming, and stayed close to his father's tents.

One day after a hunting trip, Esau was tired and hungry and asked Jacob for some lentils he was cooking. But Jacob was cunning and greedy, and offered to sell Esau some food in return for his birthright. As the oldest son, Esau, was entitled to most of his father's possessions when he died. But he was careless, and didn't worry about his future birthright, and agreed to sell it to Jacob for some food.

One day Isaac, who had grown nearly blind and weak, knew he was dying, and wanted to bless his eldest son, and give him the birthright. He sent for Esau and asked him to shoot a buck, and cook some venison for him.

Rebekah's favourite was Jacob, and when she heard this, she went to Jacob with a cunning plan. Jacob was to kill two kids from his flock of goats, and she would

then make a tasty dish for Isaac, and because he was nearly blind, he would bless Jacob instead of Esau.

Jacob was worried, not because the trick was dishonest, but because Isaac usually touched people to tell who they were, and might recognise him because of his smooth skin. But Rebekah tied goats skins onto the back of Jacob's hands, and neck.

Isaac liked the dish, but was suspicious, because he could not understand how Esau could have brought the meat so quickly.

Jacob, however, told him that God had brought a buck to him as soon as he had left the camp.

Isaac was still suspicious, and even when he felt the goats hair on the back of his son's hands he said: "The voice is Jacob's voice, but the hands are hairy like Esau's."

Then Jacob said: "I am your son Esau", and Isaac blessed him and asked God to give his son fruitful fields, and rain to make his crops grow, and plenty of corn and wine. He asked God to make his son into a great man, so that even his own brothers would bow down to him.

Jacob had hardly left Isaac's tent when Esau arrived with the savoury venison he had cooked for his father.

When Esau told his father what had happened, the poor old man was very upset. "I have blessed him and I cannot take back that blessing!" he said.

Then Isaac blessed Esau as well, and told him that his dwelling-place would be away from the fruitful

fields, where no dew falls from heaven. "You will have to live by the sword, and serve your brother, but one day you will shake off his rule," Isaac told him.

Esau hated Jacob for what he had done, and planned to kill him, but he would not do so while his father was alive. Rebekah learnt of this, and told Jacob to go away to Haran to find a wife, and even persuaded Isaac to give him his blessing before he left. It was fourteen years before Jacob was to return.

Esau was so angry that in defiance he married Hittite women from Canaan, and an Israelite.

One night on his journey to Haran, Jacob was sleeping with a stone for his pillow when he dreamt that he saw a ladder reaching from earth to heaven, with angels going up and down. At the top was the Lord who promised Jacob that all the country round about would be his and his children's after him.

Jacob was afraid and took the stone he had used as a pillow and made an altar and called the place Beth-el, the "House of God".

After a long journey, Jacob reached Haran, and there he met in a field one of the daughters of Laban, who was looking after her father's sheep. Her name was Rachel, and Jacob fell in love with her at once. When he went home with her, Laban welcomed him with joy, and told Jacob that he could stay with them. Each day Jacob helped with the sheep; and after a month, Laban asked him what he would like as a reward. Jacob wanted Rachel to be his wife, and he

was willing even to work for seven years to have her as his own!

Those seven years seemed like only a few days, Jacob loved Rachel so much. But at the end of them, Laban tricked him! He gave him Leah, Rachel's elder sister instead; and he had to serve for seven years more to get Rachel as his second wife. But he loved her so much that he was even willing to do that!

In the end they were happily married; and after a few years Jacob felt that he must go home again. By now he and his wives had eleven sons, and they were a large and rich family. Slowly they moved from Haran towards Canaan, where Jacob had lived. But he was afraid. He still remembered how he had tricked Esau, and he wondered what his brother would do to him.

He sent messengers on ahead, to tell Esau that he was coming, and to offer him a present. But they came back to report that Esau was coming out to meet him with four hundred men. That terrified Jacob. Oh, how he pleaded with God in prayer to help him!

That night he sent ahead some of his servants with a large number of cattle and sheep and camels and asses, to give them to Esau to take away his anger. Then he himself stayed alone across the brook Jabbok, to pray.

And there a mysterious man came to wrestle with him – but it was not really a man: it was the Angel of the Lord Himself! Right until the dawning of the new day they struggled there, till the Angel touched

Jacob's thigh, and he was made lame. But still Jacob would not let go, until the Angel blessed him.

This was the blessing: "Your name is no longer Jacob, 'trickster'. From now on you are Israel, 'Prince of God', because you have wrestled with God and not been defeated." From that night on, Israel limped until the end of his life.

The next morning the brothers met. Esau threw his arms around Jacob and kissed him – not at all what Jacob had expected or deserved. And he would not take the gift of cattle and sheep either.

After they had feasted together, Esau went back to his home near Mount Seir, and Israel made a home for himself and his family at Succoth. At last there was peace between the brothers.

JOSEPH THE DREAMER

Joseph was one of twelve sons and the favourite of his father Jacob, a chief in the land of Canaan. Although Benjamin, his youngest brother looked up to him, his other brothers disliked him because he bragged and carried tales, and their anger turned to hate when their father gave Joseph a coat of many colours.

When Joseph told them about two dreams he had had, they were even more angry. In one he dreamt they were all binding corn, and his sheaf stood upright while the others bowed down before it. In the second dream, the sun, the moon and eleven stars, bowed down before him.

His elder brothers guessed the meaning of the dream, and even his father said: "Shall I and your mother and brothers bow down to you, my son?"

One day Joseph was sent to visit his brothers who had taken their flocks away to find fresh grass. They stripped off his coat, and threw him into a deep pit, and when some merchants came by on their way to Egypt, Joseph's brother Judah suggested that they should sell him for twenty pieces of silver.

They then dipped his coat in the blood of a young goat, and when Jacob saw the coat, he was sure his son had been killed by a wild beast.

Joseph was sold in Egypt as a slave to Potiphar, an officer of Pharaoh, who ruled Egypt. At first he was angry at his brothers' treachery, but then he remembered the tales he had carried about them, and how boastful he had been, and he asked God to forgive him.

Joseph worked hard for Potiphar, who put him in charge of his house, and all went well until Potiphar's wife told him lies about Joseph.

He was thrown into prison, but he prayed for help, and God answered by letting the prison keeper know Joseph could be trusted, and he was put in charge of the other prisoners.

One day Joseph helped a prisoner who had been Pharaoh's butler by explaining a dream he could not understand. Joseph told him that Pharaoh would give him back his job, and he implored the man to tell Pharaoh about his plight.

The butler returned to Pharaoh and two years later, when Pharaoh had a strange dream he could not understand, the butler remembered Joseph, and Pharaoh had him brought before him.

Washed, and wearing clean clothes, Joseph bowed before the King. Pharaoh told him about his dream in which seven fat cows were eaten by seven lean cows, but they became no fatter than they were before, and seven plump ears of grain growing on one stalk were swallowed by seven thin ears.

Joseph prayed to God for guidance because he

knew Pharaoh's magicians had been unable to explain the dream. Then he said that God was showing Pharaoh what he was going to do. The dream meant that there would be seven years of plenty in the land, followed by seven years of famine, and Pharaoh should find a wise man he could trust to store up the corn in the years of plenty, so that the people would not starve in the years of famine.

Pharaoh knew what Joseph meant, and said to him: "Since God has shown you all this, there is no one as wise as you are, and you shall be in charge of all the land of Egypt, second only to me."

Joseph married, and had two sons, and during the next seven years he worked hard preparing for the famine. When it came, only Egypt had plenty of food, and people came from countries all around to buy corn from Joseph.

Back in Canaan, Joseph's family was hungry, and Jacob sent his sons to Egypt to buy grain, but he kept Benjamin at home.

Joseph recognised his brothers as they bowed down before him, and as they did not recognise him, he pretended to think they were spies. Anxious to know if they had become better men he asked many questions, and was overjoyed to learn his father was well.

Then to prove they were honest men, and not spies, he made Simeon stay behind, and told them to take

the grain back to Canaan, and return with their youngest brother, Benjamin.

Joseph ordered his servants to fill his brothers' bags with grain, and put the money they had paid on top. That night the brothers found the gold, and were terrified. They told Jacob what had happened, but he refused to let them take Benjamin.

But, when the corn was all eaten, he gave them presents, and double the money they had found in the sacks, and agreed to allow Benjamin to accompany them back to Egypt.

Joseph was overjoyed to see Benjamin, and longed to tell his brothers who he was, but he wanted to make sure they were really better men, and planned to test them.

He had his silver cup hidden in Benjamin's sack of grain, and when they set out for home, he sent his soldiers after them to arrest Benjamin, and bring him back to him.

But his brothers cried out: "Our father has already lost his favourite son Joseph; if we go back without Benjamin he will die of a broken heart."

When Judah offered to change places with Benjamin, Joseph knew his brothers had become good, unselfish men.

"Do not grieve for what you did," he told them. "God meant me to come here and save life in Egypt." Then he sent them back to Canaan and told them to bring their father and their families back with them.

When Jacob heard what Joseph had said, and he saw the food and the wagons Pharaoh had sent to take them back to Egypt, he knew Joseph was alive.

As Jacob and his family reached the Egyptian province of Goshen, Joseph rode out in a chariot to meet them. He wept tears of joy when he saw the old man, and settled his family in the best part of Egypt, and put his brothers in charge of the cattle, as Pharaoh had said.

Joseph remained Governor of Egypt during the terrible years of famine. The people offered money, cattle, horses and even land in exchange for corn, and everything he took from the people he gave to Pharaoh.

Then Joseph gave them seed, and told them to give a fifth of their harvest to Pharaoh, and keep the rest. The people agreed saying: "You have saved our lives; we will become Pharaoh's servants."

Jacob lived in Egypt for seventeen years, and was a very old man when he died.

Joseph told his brothers before he died: "God will visit you and bring you out of this land, and you shall carry my bones into Canaan."

So Joseph's great life came to an end at the age of one hundred and ten.

THE BABY IN THE BASKET

About three hundred years after Joseph's death, a cruel Pharaoh ruled Egypt, who made slaves of the Hebrews, or Israelites. When he ordered soldiers to kill all the baby boys, one Hebrew mother, called Amram, wove a basket of bulrushes, and putting her baby son in the basket, she hid it among the bulrushes at the edge of the River Nile.

Amram's daughter Miriam was watching over the baby, when Pharaoh's daughter found the basket, and seeing the baby, knew he must be a Hebrew.

Miriam asked the princess to let her find a Hebrew woman to nurse the child, and when she returned with Amram, the princess told her: "Take this child away, and nurse him and, I will pay you."

When the baby was older, he was taken to the palace, and adopted by the princess as her son, and given the name of Moses, which meant he had been taken out of the water.

He became an Egyptian prince, and was taught to read and write, and learnt about the heathen gods and goddesses worshipped by the Egyptians. But his Hebrew parents also told him about the Lord God, Jehovah.

One day Moses went to the aid of the seven daughters of a priest of Midian called Jethro, when some shepherds chased away their sheep from the local well.

When they reached home, and their father heard what had happened, he told his daughters to fetch Moses, and invite him to a meal. Moses accepted Jethro's invitation to live with the family and help look after the sheep, and later on he married Jethro's daughter, Zipporah, and they had a son named Gershom.

When the King of Egypt died, the children of Israel, unable to bear their cruel treatment any longer, cried out for God's help.

God took pity of them, and one day, as Moses was grazing Jethro's sheep, he was puzzled to see a bush alight with a fire that did not burn out. Then suddenly, from the bush, he heard the voice of God telling him that he must go back to his own people in Goshen, and tell them that God had sent him to lead them to freedom into a land so rich it "flowed with milk and honey."

Moses was afraid the Hebrew people would not believe him, so God promised he should have the power to do miracles to prove he had been sent by God. He also promised that his brother Aaron should help him.

So Moses went back to Egypt and with his brother, Aaron, they gathered together the elders and people of

Israel, but the Israelites still could not believe that their days of slavery would be coming to an end, until Moses, using the power that God had promised him, started to do miracles. He threw down a stick and it became a snake. When he caught the snake by its tail, it turned back into a stick. Then he put his hand in his tunic and when he pulled it out it was white with leprosy, when he put it back and took it out again, it was healthy.

When the Hebrews saw these miracles they believed Moses, and bowed and worshipped God.

Moses and his brother then went to Pharaoh and asked him to let the Hebrews free to go into the desert to worship. But Pharaoh refused, and made life even harder for the Hebrews. Then God brought plagues down upon Egypt, but they hurt only the Egyptians, not the Israelites.

The first plague came as Pharaoh was going to bathe in the River Nile. Moses and Aaron again warned the king to release the slaves, and when he refused, Moses hit the water so that it turned into blood. The fish died, and the water became foul, and for seven days the Egyptians could not drink it, and they had to dig holes for drinking water. Still Pharaoh would not listen, so God sent a plague of frogs. Pharaoh told Moses and Aaron that if God would take away the frogs he would do as God demanded, but when the frogs disappeared, Pharaoh broke his promise.

Then God sent a plague of gnats, and then a plague

of flies, but as soon as God took away the plagues, Pharaoh again went back on his word.

So the plagues went on. After the flies came a plague on cattle; and a plague of hail and storms, but still Pharaoh would not give in.

When a plague of locusts settled over Egypt, and ate all the plants and fruits, Pharaoh promised he would keep his word if God would take away the locusts. God sent a strong west wind which blew the locusts into the Red Sea, but again Pharaoh broke his promise.

When God sent a plague of darkness which covered the land for three days, Pharaoh told Moses that he could take the Israelites, but they must leave their sheep and cattle behind. When Moses refused, Pharaoh told him that if Moses ever came near him again, he would have him put to death.

Then came the last and most terrible plague of all. God told Moses that at midnight all the first born of the land of Egypt should die, from the first born of Pharaoh, to the first born of the cattle. He told the Israelites to prepare a meal of roasted lamb and vegetables and bread without yeast, and to dip herbs in the lambs blood, and make marks on the doors of their houses. They were told to stay indoors until morning, for when God saw the blood on the houses, their inhabitants would be safe.

That night there was terror in Egypt, and all the first born sons died, and only the Israelites who had listen-

ed to God escaped the terrible touch of death.

This time Pharaoh was in a hurry to keep his promise, and told Moses to take the people of Israel and their flocks out of Egypt as quickly as he could. And so four hundred and thirty years after Jacob and his family had entered Egypt, the Children of Israel left.

With Moses at their head, six hundred thousand men, with their women and children, set out for the Red Sea. Moses took with him the bones of Joseph, Jacob's favourite son, and the Lord went before them in a pillar of cloud by day, and in a pillar of fire by night.

The Jews still keep the Passover Feast each year to remind them how God passed over the homes of their fathers in Egypt, and freed them from slavery.

When Pharaoh realised he had lost all his slaves he went after them with his soldiers and a great army of chariots. The Israelites were frightened but when they reached the Sea of Reeds God told Moses to lift his rod and stretch his hand over the sea. The waters divided and the Israelites passed safely through. When the Egyptians tried to follow, Moses again stretched out his rod, and the waters came back drowning the Egyptians.

So God saved the Israelite people, and they believed in Him and trusted His servant Moses.

MOSES THE LEADER

When God freed the Israelites from slavery in Egypt they were overjoyed, but they had to cross a barren desert where there was very little water or food.

In the daytime God led them in a pillar of cloud, and in a column of fire by night.

They followed Moses from the Red Sea to the Wilderness of Sin. For three days they went without water, and even when they reached the fountain of Marah, the water was too bitter to drink.

The people were angry, but God told Moses to throw a branch from a nearby tree into the water. At once the water became sweet enough to drink.

God warned the Israelites not to grumble, but to obey His commands, and He would take care of them.

But even when they complained that there was not enough food as they were crossing the Wilderness of Sin, God helped them by sending flocks of quails into camp for them to catch. He told them to catch enough on the sixth day to tide them over on the seventh, which was the Sabbath.

When they reached Rephidim, and found the fountain was dry, they were angry, and wanted to stone Moses to death. But God told Moses to hit the rock at

Rephidim with his staff, and when he did so, water poured out of the rock.

The Amalekites attacked the Israelites when they were at Rephidim, and, while Joshua led the Israelites in battle, Moses and Aaron and Hur stood on a nearby hill to watch.

Moses held his arms in the air, and prayed that God would give his people the victory. The battle kept on for a long time. As long as Moses kept his arms in the air, the Israelites had the upper hand; but as soon as he was tired and his arms began to drop, the Amalekites began to win. Then Aaron and Hur came and stood alongside Moses, and held his arms up, until in the end the men of Israel beat the Amalekites and drove them away.

After a long journey the Israelites came to Mount Sinai. Over the mountain hung a great cloud which hid the top of the mountain. The Israelites were told not to come near the mountain, nor touch it, because it was God's sacred mountain. They had to stay on the plain below, and wash themselves and their clothes, and get ready to hear a special message from God.

When three days had passed, they heard peals of thunder and sounds like a trumpet coming from the cloud. There was also lightning. The people were afraid, but Moses lead them out of their camp to a place at the foot of the mountain. Then God called Moses from out of the cloud. He climbed the slopes of the mountain, and disappeared into the cloud.

There in the cloud, God gave to Moses the Laws which are still our laws today. We call them the Ten Commandments.

Here they are: "I am the Lord your God, Who brought you out of the land of Egypt, out of the house of bondage. You shall have no other gods beside Me. You shall not make for yourself a graven image nor the likeness of anything that is in heaven above, nor that is in the earth beneath, nor that is in the water under the earth: you shall not bow yourself down to them nor serve them: for I the Lord your God am a jealous God, visiting the iniquity of the fathers on the children, unto the third and fourth generations of those that hate Me; and showing mercy to thousands of them that love Me, and keep My commandments. You shall not take the name of the Lord your God in vain; for the Lord will not hold him guiltless that takes His name in vain. Remember the sabbath day to keep it holy. Six days you shall labour, and do all your work; but the seventh day is a sabbath to the Lord your God: in it you shall not do any work, you, nor your son, nor your daughter, your manservant, nor your maidservant, nor your cattle, nor the stranger that is within your gates: for in six days the Lord made heaven and earth, the sea, and all that in them is, and rested the seventh day: wherefore the Lord blessed the sabbath day, and hallowed it. Honour your father and your mother that your days may be long in the land which the Lord your God gives to you. You shall do no murder. You shall

not commit adultery. You shall not steal. You shall not bear false witness against your neighbour. You shall not covet your neighbour's wife, nor his manservant, nor his maidservant, nor his ox, nor his ass, nor anything that is your neighbour's.''

God also made a promise to the Israelites. He would send His Angel to lead them through the desert and into the land of Canaan. That was the land which He had promised to them.

Moses stayed on the mountain-top for forty days. The people wondered what had happened to him; then they did something terrible. They went to Moses' brother, Aaron, and asked him to make them idols which they could worship. He made them a golden calf out of the earrings and other treasures they brought to him.

When Moses came down from the mountain, he saw an awful thing. Aaron had called a feast day for the Lord, but he and many of the people were burning sacrifices before the golden calf! Moses was furious when he saw that, so furious that he threw the stone tablets on which God's Law was written, onto the ground.

The tablets broke in pieces. Moses rushed up and took the golden calf and threw it into a fire. Then he called all the people who were faithful to God and would not have anything to do with the idol. All the rest were put to death for their terrible sin: there were about three thousand of them altogether.

After this Moses went back into the cloud on the mountain-top and asked God to forgive the Israelites for their sin. And God forgave them.

RUTH AND NAOMI

Long ago, when the judges ruled Israel, the crops failed and there was a terrible famine. One Israelite called Elimelech, took his wife, Naomi, and their two sons to live in Moab on the other side of the Dead Sea.

When Elimelech died his sons married two Moabite women Orpah and Ruth, and for ten years Naomi lived with them, but when both sons died, Naomi decided to return to Israel, because the famine there had ended.

Orpah and Ruth loved Naomi, and decided to keep her company on the journey, until she crossed the River Jordan into Israel.

Eventually Orpah tearfully started home, but Ruth refused to leave Naomi, and said she would make Naomi's people her people, and their God her God.

When they both reached Bethlehem they soon found somewhere to live, and as the harvest was just beginning, and they needed food, Ruth went to the fields, according to custom, to gather the stalks of corn left behind by the reapers.

One day Ruth was gathering corn in a field belonging to Boaz, a rich relative of Naomi's husband who had died, when he enquired who she was.

When they told him, Boaz spoke kindly to Ruth,

and told her to keep close to his reapers. "I have told my young men not to bother you and to let you drink from our drinking pots," he said.

Ruth fell on the ground, and asked why he was showing such kindness to her, a foreigner. But Boaz told her that he knew of the kindness she had shown to Naomi, adding: "The Lord God of Israel will not forget you, and will reward you for what you have done."

When it was time to eat, Boaz told Ruth to sit with the reapers, to share some of their bread with them, and even dip it in the same dish of sauce with them. He even sat down with them, and passed handfuls of parched corn to her to enjoy. There was so much that she was able even to keep some, and to take it home to Naomi.

In the afternoon, when Ruth went back to her gleaning, Boaz told his reapers to pull some barley out of the bundles, and to drop handfuls on purpose for her to pick up.

Ruth worked in the field until evening, and when she had beaten out the husks to get the grain, there was a great deal to take home to Naomi, as well as the parched corn left over from the midday meal.

Naomi was surprised to see so much. "Where have you been working today to gather such a lot of grain?" she asked.

Ruth told her everything that had happened, and the name of the friendly man in whose fields she had worked.

"That man, Boaz, is a relative of ours," Naomi said excitedly. "This is the Lord's own doing. May the Lord bless him for his kindness."

Every day until the end of the barley and the wheat harvests, Ruth gleaned in the fields belonging to Boaz. In this way she was able to collect enough food to make sure she and Naomi would have enough to keep them right through the coming winter.

Now the Israelites had a custom, that if a man died without leaving children and he owned land, the nearest relative had the right to buy that land, and marry the widow. When Elimelech lived in Bethlehem, before the famine, he had owned a piece of land there. Something had to be done about that land.

One day Naomi said to Ruth: "My daughter, it is time you had a home of your own; and Boaz, our relative can help you. Tonight he will be working on the threshing floor, separating the chaff from the barley. Wash and put on your best clothes, and go and see him there. Wait until he has finished his supper, and then when he lies down to sleep, find a place near him where you can lie down as well. When he notices you and speaks to you, tell him all about your troubles."

So that evening Ruth put on her best clothes, and went down to the threshing floor as her mother-in-law had told her. She waited until Boaz had finished eating and drinking. When he lay down to sleep on a heap of

the straw from the threshing, she wrapped herself in her cloak, and lay down at his feet. Some time after midnight, Boaz stirred in his sleep, and woke up. How surprised he was to see a woman lying at his feet. In the dark he could not recognise her. "Who are you?" he called out. "I am Ruth, your servant," she answered, "but now I am troubled, and I need your help. You are related to me by marriage."

"I will do all that I can, because I know you are a good woman," said Boaz. "It is also true that I am a relative of yours, but there is a man who is a still nearer relative than I am. Tomorrow morning I will go and see him, and if he is not willing to do his duty by you, then I promise that, as the Lord lives, I shall. Now do not worry, but rest until morning."

In the morning, while it was still dark, Ruth prepared to go back home, but Boaz insisted on filling the sheet on which she had slept with six measures of barley for her to take back to Naomi.

The following day Boaz went to see Ruth's nearest relative, and sat down with him at the gate of the town of Bethlehem, and invited ten elders of the city to join them.

When Boaz explained the position to the man, and told him that it was his right to buy the land which had belonged to Elimelech, he agreed to do so.

But when Boaz also reminded the man that part of the bargain would be for him to marry Ruth, the

Moabitess, he refused, and told Boaz that he must take the right for himself.

Then the man pulled off one of his sandals and gave it to Boaz, to indicate that he was giving Boaz the right to take his place in buying the land, and marrying Ruth.

Boaz asked the elders to be witness, and all the people were so pleased to know that Boaz would be marrying Ruth, whom he loved dearly, that they cried out: "May you prosper and become famous in Bethlehem, and may the Lord bless you and your new wife with many children."

After the marriage Naomi lived quietly in Bethlehem, and when a son was born to Boaz and Ruth, she took him in her arms and kissed him, and became his nurse.

The child was named Obed, and he became the father of Jesse, the grandfather of King David, and one of the forefathers of our precious Saviour, Jesus Christ.

SAMSON

Because the Israelites fell into bad ways, God punished them by letting the Philistines rule over them for forty years.

The Philistines were clever, and knew how to make iron which in those days made them very powerful, because they could forge the finest and strongest weapons of war, and produce the best farming equipment.

Whilst they ruled Israel, a baby was born who was to be the thirteenth judge to rule Israel, and the strongest man in the world.

Before he was born an angel visited his mother, the wife of Manoah, who told her that she would have a baby son who would free the Israelites from the Philistines, but she must eat only foods which were clean, and must not drink wine or strong drink, and must never cut the child's hair.

When she told her husband, Manoah, that they would have a son, he also prayed that he might see the angel, and know how to treat the child.

Soon afterwards the angel appeared again, and told Manoah that he must see that his wife did all the angel said, and never cut the hair of their son's head.

As God had promised they had a son whom they

called Samson, and he grew strong, and the Lord blessed him in all that he did.

Although his parents obeyed the angel, and saw that he was strictly brought up, Samson was rather inclined to do whatever he wanted, and one day, to his parents distress, he fell in love with a Philistine girl from Timnath.

They begged Samson not to marry a Philistine because they were their enemies, but when they saw that he loved her very much, they set out to visit her home.

It was a long journey and on the way Samson was attacked by a lion, but he was not afraid because he knew the Lord was with him, and rolling over and over on the dusty road with the great beast, he killed it with his bare hands.

His parents were some way off, and not wishing to frighten them, he said nothing of his fight with the lion.

When they arrived at Timnath arrangements were made for the wedding, and although Samson was an Israelite the girl's parents were pleased for her to marry Samson, because his great strength was known throughout the land.

The feasting lasted many days, and the Philistine guests were puzzled by a riddle Samson asked of them, saying if they could find the answer he would give them each a set of new clothes, and if they were unable to do so they should each give him a set of clothes.

For three days the guests tried to solve the riddle

and eventually they persuaded Samson's bride to get the answer from her husband. When Samson heard that his wife had told the answer to the Philistines he was very angry, and went out and killed 30 Philistines from a nearby city.

He did not return home until after the harvest, and when he arrived her father barred the door to him, saying that she had married another man because she thought that Samson hated her too much after what she had done.

This made Samson even more angry, and he set his heart against the Philistines for ever. At one time he tied burning torches to the tails of 300 foxes and drove them into the vinyards and fields belonging to the Philistines, so that their crops were burnt and there was no harvest.

The Philistines bound Samson with a strong new rope, but he burst his bonds, and picked up the jawbone of an ass and killed one thousand men in his anger.

After this he settled down, and for twenty years became a judge among the Israelites.

The Philistines did not forget, however, and one day when he was in the city of Gaza they closed the city gates, and planned to kill him. Samson learnt of their trap, and at midnight he crept out, and with a mighty heave pulled up the gates and the posts and carried them shoulder high to a high hill.

The Philistines were stunned and afraid, and said

among themselves: "We must find out the hidden secret of this man's great strength". They turned to a woman called Delilah whom Samson loved even though she too was a Philistine. At first she refused to help, but when they offered her eleven hundred pieces of silver, she agreed to betray the man who loved her.

Whenever Delilah saw Samson, she tried to find out why he was so strong, but always he refused to answer the question, until one day, he was so tormented by her continually asking him, that he told her all:

"No one must ever put a razor to my head, for God said if my hair was shaved, I would lose all my strength, and become weak."

As soon as Delilah heard this, she hurried to the Philistines, and told them what Samson had said to her. They gave her the silver which they had promised, and at once set out to destroy the great strength of Samson.

One day while Samson was sleeping, Delilah called for a Philistine to come and shave off Samson's hair while he slept. Straight away a man came and did this, and when he awoke, Samson's strength had gone.

Then the Philistines took him away, put heavy chains of brass on his arms and legs, and put out his eyes, making poor Samson blind.

One day soon after, the Philistines gathered together in a great temple to give thanks to their god, Dagon, and to celebrate the capture of Samson. All the important Philistines were there, men and women,

and the lords of the Philistines. About three thousand sang, danced and drank wine, and while all this was going on, Samson was brought before them, so that they could laugh at the helpless blind man, who had once been so strong.

A young boy led Samson into the temple, for he was not able to see. The Philistines were so busy enjoying themselves that they did not notice Samson's hair had grown while he had been in prison. He turned to the boy and said: "Let me feel the pillars so that I may know where I am." So the young lad gently placed one of his hands on each pillar. Then with a loud voice, Samson called out to God, saying: "Oh! Lord God remember me. Oh God! May I be avenged for the loss of my eyes. Let me die now with the Philistines." And Samson pushed with all his strength until the great pillars gave way. They crashed to the ground with a mighty roar. The whole place trembled and the walls and roof fell down on the people, killing everyone; and under the pillars, too, lay Samson – dead.

SAMUEL, THE LAST JUDGE

The families of Israel visited Shiloh each year, because God's Ten Commandments were kept there inside the Ark of the Lord.

Among them was a woman called Hannah, who so longed for a son, that at last she cried out to God saying: "If Thou wilt give me a son, I will lend him to Thee all the days of his life."

When Eli the priest heard this promise he said to her: "Go in peace, the God of Israel will answer your prayers."

Soon afterwards Hannah had a son whom she called Samuel. Hannah and her husband, Elkanah, loved their son, but when he was old enough to leave home, Hannah took Samuel to the temple and told Eli the priest: "The Lord has answered my prayer, and now I will lend my son to God for as long as he lives."

Eli took the child, after they had prayed together, and his parents returned home to Ramah.

Samuel grew to love the priest, and each year his parents came to visit him, and brought him a little coat.

As the years passed Samuel grew wiser and everyone loved and respected him, especially Eli

whose own two sons had been a disappointment to him.

One evening when Samuel was lying down in the temple, he heard a voice saying: "Samuel!". Samuel, thinking that Eli had called him, ran to him saying: "Here I am." But Eli sent him back to bed saying: "I did not call."

Three times Samuel heard the voice. On the third time Eli knew that it must be the Lord calling Samuel and told him that if the Lord called again he should reply: "Speak Lord, for Thy servant hears Thee."

When the Lord called again he told Samuel that he would do a thing in Israel at which both ears of everyone that heard it would tingle, and that he had told Eli that he would punish his whole family because of his sons' wicked ways.

Samuel was at first afraid to tell Eli, but when he did Eli answered: "It is the Lord's word; let Him do what seems good in His sight."

The Lord was with Samuel as he grew into a young man, and everyone listened to his wise words, knowing that he was a judge, and a prophet chosen by God.

During the battle between the Israelites and the Philistines, four thousand soldiers of Israel were killed and the people began to lose hope.

Then they thought of a plan to carry the Ark before them into battle, and when the Israelite soldiers saw the Ark, they gave a loud cry. So great was their shout that the Philistines became afraid, and seeing the Ark,

believed that God had come down to fight against them.

But the leaders of the Philistines called them together, and in the terrible fighting that took place they killed thirty thousand Israelites including the sons of Eli, and took from them the Ark of the Lord.

When Eli heard that the Philistines had taken the Ark and killed his two sons the old man fell down dead.

After the Philistines had captured the ark, they had so many troubles because they were afraid of it. Everywhere they took it, there was illness, death and destruction, so they decided amongst themselves to return the ark to the land of Israel. They made a cart, and placed the ark on it, and carried golden ornaments to put on each side of it – hoping that they would be forgiven. When they were ready, they put two cows in front to pull the cart, and sent it on its way.

As soon as the cart left the Philistines, the cows headed straight for the land of Israel. They did not stop until they reached a field, where there were some people harvesting. When these people saw the ark of the Lord, they were beside themselves with joy, and at once they built an altar, and placed the ark on it.

Now that Eli was dead, Samuel became judge over all Israel, and said to the people: "Return to your Lord. Do not worship other gods. Serve Him only, and God will free you from the Philistines."

And so Samuel travelled from city to city helping

people to solve their problems, and giving his advice in all matters.

When at last he became old, the chief men of the temple begged him to appoint a king to rule over them. At first he did not agree, because he was afraid that a king would demand too much of his people, but God called and said to him: "Listen to them, Samuel. Find them a king..."

Now there lived in the village of Gibeah a young man called Saul. He was a fine-looking Israelite, and taller than any other man in the land. His father, Kish, a very rich landowner, was indeed proud of his only son.

One day some of their asses went astray, and Kish sent Saul and a servant in search of them. As they were near Ramah, the home of Samuel, they decided to call on him, thinking that he could tell them where to look for their lost asses. They, like all the people, knew that Samuel was a seer (this means a man who knows what is going to happen in the future) and therefore they were sure that he would help them.

It was a very strange thing for Saul to call on Samuel, for only the day before God had spoken to Samuel saying: "Tomorrow at this hour, I will send to you a man from the tribe of Benjamin – you shall make him a king, and he will save my people from the Philistines."

When Samuel saw this tall Israelite coming towards him, he heard God again saying: "This is he whom I have

chosen to rule over my people," and at once Samuel went to Saul and asked him to come into his house.

When it was morning, they arose, and Samuel walked with Saul and his servant to a quiet place, then suddenly he said that he wanted to spend a while with Saul, and the servant went ahead leaving his master with Samuel. When they were alone, Samuel filled a horn with holy oil, and poured it upon Saul's head, saying: "I anoint you in the name of the Lord. You will be king over all Israel, and save us from the hands of our enemies."

Saul could not believe what was happening. It had come as such a surprise, but as he felt the oil pouring over him, he knew that he must do God's work. Then Samuel called the people together at a place called Mizpah and showed Saul to them saying: "Here is the man chosen by God to be your king." At once a great shout went up: "God save the king – Long live the king!"

And so it was, that Samuel, the last judge to rule over Israel, showed to the great multitude of the people of Israel, Saul, their first king.

DAVID AND GOLIATH

Although David, the son of Jesse, was only a shepherd boy, who loved looking after his father's sheep in the green hills of Bethlehem, he loved beautiful things. He sat among the trees watching the birds and animals, the moon and stars and sky.

Sometimes he sat with his lyre among the flowers singing songs about God's goodness to his people.

One of his best known songs was the 23rd. Psalm which we still sing to-day:

"The Lord is my shepherd; I shall not want.
He maketh me to lie down in green pastures:
He leadeth me beside the still waters.
He restoreth my soul:
He leadeth me in the paths of
righteousness for His name's sake.
Yea, though I walk through the valley
of the shadow of death,
I will fear no evil: for Thou are with me;
Thy rod and Thy staff they comfort me.
Thou preparest a table before me in the
presence of mine enemies.
Thou anointest my head with oil;
my cup runneth over.

Surely goodness and mercy shall follow
me all the days of my life.
And I will dwell in the house of the
Lord for ever."

In those days God was not very pleased with Saul,
the King of Israel, and told Samuel, the prophet, to go
to the house of Jesse, to find the man he had chosen to
be king.

When Samuel reached the house of Jesse in
Bethlehem, and saw his seven strong, fine looking
sons, he picked out Eliab, because he was so tall and
noble in appearance.

But God told Samuel to look further than the face
or height of a man, saying, "It is what is in a man's
heart that is the most important thing."

Samuel asked Jesse to send for his youngest son
David, who was in the hills looking after the sheep,
and when Samuel saw David, the voice of God told
him: "This is the one that I have chosen. Arise! Anoint
him."

Then Samuel took the horn, and filling it with holy
oil, poured it on the head of David. From that moment
the Spirit of the Lord entered David, the shepherd boy
who would one day be king.

Although Saul was a brave warrior, he suffered
terrible moments of madness. A servant, remembering how well David played and sang, sent for him.

Saul liked David, and whenever he played his lyre,
and sang, he felt calm and rested. He made David his

armour-bearer, and when he went into battle, David carried Saul's sword, shield, and spear.

He did not know that Samuel had anointed David, and that one day he could be king, or he would have been very jealous.

When Saul seemed better, David was sent back to his father, and once again tended the sheep, and played and sang the songs we now call: "The Psalms of David."

One day David's father sent him to see whether three of his brothers were safe who had joined Saul's army against the Philistines.

When David arrived the two armies were in camps on either side of the valley of Elah. Each day Goliath, the champion warrior of the Philistines, used to roar across to the Israelites: "Choose a man to come and fight me, If he kills me we will become servants of Israel. If I kill him, then you will serve us."

The Israelites hated war, and had few weapons, and even so no one dared fight Goliath, who was nine feet tall, and carried a spear which was twice the size of any other soldiers. He wore a suit of armour, and a helmet of brass.

Although his brothers tried to disuade him, David asked to see the King, because he was sure he knew of a way to kill the giant.

The king had promised his daughter to whoever could kill the giant, along with a high position in his army, but David was not interested in the rewards, he

just wanted to rid his people of this terrible Philistine.

At first King Saul did not recognise the boy who had been his armour-bearer, because he had grown so much, and refused to let him fight the giant.

But David told him: "One day a lion and a bear took a lamb from my father's flock, and I went after them, and killed the lion and the bear, and took the lamb from the lion's jaws. The Lord protected me, and I know the Lord will be with me if I fight Goliath."

When Saul saw that David was not afraid, he offered David his armour and sword, but David refused, and collecting five smooth stones, he put them in his shepherd's bag. Carrying his staff, and sling, he went forward to meet the giant.

When the Philistine saw that David was a young man, he said: "I wil kill you, and give your body to the birds of the air, and the beasts of the fields."

But David replied bravely: "You have come to me with sword and spear, but I come to you in the name of the Lord. Today He will deliver you into my hands."

Goliath rose up in a mighty rage, and drew near to David, his armour clanking as he strode towards the shepherd boy, who looked calm and unafraid.

Goliath raised his mighty sword, but still David stood firm. "Am I a dog that you come at me with a staff?" shouted the angry Goliath.

Just then David took a step or two forward, and he seemed to be looking to see which way the wind was blowing; his hands quickly took out one of the smooth

stones from the leather bag, and placed it in his sling.

At that moment, Goliath came lumbering towards him, his sword waving madly in the air. He was almost upon David, when suddenly David took aim, and the stone from the sling sped through the air, and hit Goliath on the forehead.

So straight and true was David's aim, that Goliath crashed to the ground – dead. It seemed that the very earth trembled as he fell. Then David ran towards the great giant, stood astride his massive body, and cut off his head with a single blow.

When the Philistines saw that their champion was dead, they fled back to their own land, and the Israelites followed them, killing thousands of the soldiers even as they reached the gates of their own city of Gath.

When David went to Saul with the head of Goliath, he was at once given a high position in the army of the Israelites.

And so it was that David, the shepherd boy from Bethlehem, son of Jesse, married the daughter of Saul, and became a great warrior – fighting and winning battles against the Philistines; and one day as God had said, David became King of all Israel.

DAVID AND JONATHAN

After David had killed Goliath and become a soldier in King Saul's army, he became great friends with Jonathan, Saul's son.

Jonathan gave David his robe and sword and bow as a sign of friendship, and they became as brothers.

King Saul loved David as a son, but in time he knew that David was an even greater soldier than he was, and his love turned to jealousy.

One day, when David was playing on his harp for the King, Saul threatened to kill David, and threw his javelin at him, but God was with David, and he avoided the sharp spear.

Jonathan begged his father not to harm David, and Saul was ashamed when he remembered how David had killed Goliath, and he sent for him, so that they might live in peace as before.

But an evil spirit attacked Saul's heart, and again he threw his javelin at David. But this time David ran to the house where he lived with his wife Michal, who was Saul's daughter.

Saul knew where David would go, and sent men to fetch him, but as they waited outside, Michal helped David escape through a window at night.

In the morning when the men came to take David,

his wife placed a pillow in the bed, and covered it with a cloth. Pointing to it Michal said: "My husband is sick, you cannot take him."

When Saul heard that his men had been fooled by his daughter, he was very angry. Jonathan was greatly disturbed at his father's action, and tried to find David to comfort him.

Jonathan told David he would help him, and when David said: "Tomorrow is the new moon, and it is my duty as a soldier of your father, and as a son-in-law, to sit by Saul's side." Jonathan replied that he would see whether Saul noticed the empty seat. If he did, and felt kindly towards David, he would let him know that he could return; but if Saul still felt angry, he would help David escape.

As a means of getting a message to David, Jonathan said he would go to a nearby field with a lad to practice his bow and arrow. While David hid behind a pile of stones, Jonathan would shoot three arrows into the air, and send the boy to fetch them. If he told the lad "The arrows are on this side of you!" it would be safe for David to return. If not, he would tell the lad: "Look the arrows are beyond you!" and David had to run and hide.

On the third day of the great feast, Saul asked for David to be found, so that he could be put to death. Hearing this Jonathan warned David using the signal they had arranged with the arrows. David knew he must run, but before doing so he and Jonathan wept together.

Saul took three thousand men to search for David, and one night they were so close that David crept with another man into the place where Saul was sleeping, and cut a piece of cloth from Saul's robe.

When they had gone far from the place where Saul slept, David shouted: "My lord! Why do you think I want to do you harm? Why should I want to kill you?" And David held up the piece of cloth, which he had just cut from Saul's robe. "You can see from this that I wish you no harm."

Saul was very sorry, for he had treated David very cruelly, and he knew David could have killed him while he slept.

"You are a better man than I am!" Saul called to David. "You have done only good things to me, and I have always treated you badly."

Though Saul said this, David could not believe that he would mean it for long, so he went back into hiding.

David was right, for once again Saul began to hunt for him; and when his camp was near, David arose again in the night, and went to Saul's sleeping place. David took with him a famous spearsman called Abishai, and they entered the camp together.

When Abishai saw the king asleep, he lifted his spear and said to David: "Let me kill Saul." But David did not want to shed blood. "Let us take this water jug, and his spear," he said. They crept out of the camp, and left Saul and his guard, Abner, fast asleep.

When they had gone to a hill some way off, David

called out to Abner: "You deserve to die, for you have not guarded your master well." "Is that your voice, my son David?" called Saul.

"It is, my lord," replied David, holding up the water jug to prove that they had just left the camp.

"I have done you wrong, my son. I will never try to harm you again, please come back to me," begged Saul.

Still David was not sure, because Saul had broken his word so many times. He knew that Saul was often ill, and did not know what he was doing, so David would not go back.

It happened that fighting broke out again between the Philistines and the Israelites. In a battle, Saul was wounded by an arrow, and his three sons were killed in front of him . . . One of them was Jonathan, whom David loved. Saul did not want to be killed by the Philistines, and he asked his armour-bearer to kill him, but the poor man was afraid to do this to his King, so Saul fell on his own sword, and thrust it into himself.

Three days later a man went to David and told him that his friend Jonathan had been killed by the Philistines.

"And Saul?" asked David. "What has happened to him?"

"He is dead, too, he and his three sons," said the messenger.

All day long David wept, for he was very sad. He had loved both Jonathan and Saul, even though Saul

had treated him so badly. David took up his harp and sang a song of mourning:

"Saul and Jonathan were lovely
And pleasant in their lives,
And in their death they were not parted.
Swifter than eagles they were
And stronger than lions."

Then David called upon the Lord and asked Him what he should do, and God said: "Go back to Israel, to the land of Judah." David obeyed, and went back to his country, and became King of all Israel.

DAVID THE KING

When King Saul ruled Israel, David had to hide, because the King was jealous of his victory over the Philistines, by killing Goliath.

The people made David King when Saul died, but the men of Benjamin, the King's old tribe, made Saul's son, Ish-bosheth, King.

King Saul's former captain, Abner, who led Ish-bosheth's army, was defeated by Joab who led David's men. He fled, but in a fight he killed Joab's brother, Asahel.

When the sun set, Abner shouted to Joab: "Shall the sword devour for ever? How long must this fighting go on?"

Joab blew his trumpet to end the battle, and took news of the victory to David.

One day when Joab was away, Abner persuaded David to unite both tribes into one nation, to serve God and fight the Philistines.

Joab was furious, and murdered Abner in revenge, but when David learnt this he instructed everyone to mourn publicly for Abner, by tearing their clothes, and wearing sackcloth.

The people knew David did not want Abner killed, and that he did not mean Ish-bosheth harm. But one

day, two men brought David Ish-bosheth's head, and told him how they had murdered him in his bed, while he rested.

David was angry, and had them executed. The elders of all the tribes of Israel made David King over the whole nation, and he took 30 000 men to Jerusalem to fight the Jebusites, a hill tribe from the rocky centry of the city.

After a terrible slaughter they were driven out, and their stronghold was re-named, the city of David. A fine palace was built there by carpenters and masons sent by Hiram, King of Tyre. Shortly afterwards David defeated the Philistines, and decided to bring the Ark of God to Jerusalem. He led a great procession to fetch the Ark from Kirjath-jearim, where it was looked after by Abinadab and his sons.

Carefully lifting the Ark by poles through the rings on its sides, they placed it on a new cart. The people played instruments, and sang and danced as the Ark was taken towards Jerusalem.

At Nachon the oxen drawing the cart stumbled, and when Uzzah, one of Abinadab's sons put out his hand to steady the Ark, he dropped down dead, for God had killed Uzzah for breaking the law not to touch the sacred Ark.

The King was terrified and had the Ark carried into the house of Obed-edom. For three months God blessed Obed-edom and his family, and David

gradually lost his fear of the Ark, and brought it to Jerusalem.

He blessed the people in God's name, and gave them a cake of bread, a portion of meat, and a cake of raisins, to continue the feast in their own homes.

David asked Nathan the prophet to build a house of gold and cedarwood for the Ark, but because David was a man of war God told Nathan that the house should be built by David's son, who would be King after him.

King David longed for peace, but still the war went on, and he gained many victories over his enemies. Then one day he discovered that Jonathan, his friend, who had been killed in battle alongside his father, King Saul, and whom he had loved so dearly, had left a lame son. At once he sent out some of his servants to fetch the young man to him. David spoke kindly to Mephibosheth, for that was his name, and told him that all the lands of his grandfather, Saul, would be given back to him in memory of his father, Jonathan.

So Mephibosheth, who had been terrified when he heard that King David wanted to see him, came to live in Jerusalem, and ate at the king's table.

As the years went by many sad things happened to David and his family, but he could never have believed that the worst would come through his favourite son Absalom, a very handsome and popular young man. Absalom had been banished from the kingdom for murdering one of his brothers, but after a time

David forgave him and he returned to Jerusalem. He should have been grateful for this, but he was greedy for power.

While living in the palace, he drove about in a fine chariot, with fifty men running before him; and when he saw people waiting by the city gate for the king to judge some dispute, he would say to them: "You are certainly in the right. If only I were judge, I would do every man justice." By saying this he was hinting that David did not always judge fairly. Whenever a man came near to bow before him, Absalom would put out his hand, and take hold of him and kiss him; in this way he stole away the hearts of the people from the king, his own father.

One day Absalom asked the king's leave to go to Hebron, where he worked out a clever plot against David. He sent spies to all the men who thought well of him in all the tribes of Israel, saying: "When you hear the sound of the trumpet you shall say: 'Absalom reigns in Hebron'."

The news of this reached David and he was deeply shocked, for he had trusted Absalom completely and loved him dearly. Things were so bad that he quickly left Jerusalem with all his household. However, he ordered that the Ark of God must remain in the city.

Although there was war between David and his son, David told his commanders: "Deal gently for my sake with the young man Absalom." A great battle was fought at Ephraim and the people of Israel were

defeated by David's armies – and Absalom was killed. That made David very sad indeed; after all, Absalom was his son!

When a messenger brought David the news of his son's death, the king wept and cried: "Oh my son Absalom! Oh Absalom, my son, my son!"

David's sons were not very kind to him. When he became old and feeble, another of them, Adonijah, thought he would try to take over the throne. He too rode in a chariot with fifty men running before him, and always had everything he wanted.

But Nathan the Prophet came, and told Queen Bathsheba to tell David of Adonijah's plans; and also of her fear that Solomon would be robbed of the throne that should be his. Bathsheba did so, and the sick old king at once gave orders that Solomon was to be led forth on the king's mule, and anointed with sacred oil at once, even before his own death.

Soon after Solomon had begun his reign, he knelt before the old king who was dying, to receive his blessing. "Be thou strong and show thyself a man. Keep the commandments of the Lord God and walk in His ways," said David.

So David, ancestor of Jesus, the founder of a royal house, who won many victories during his forty-year reign over Israel, died and was buried in Jerusalem, the city which bore his own name, the City of David . .

SOLOMON THE WISE

Solomon became King of Israel when his father David died. The Kingdom was very large and peoples from many nations lived there including Israelites, Edomites, Ammonites and Syrians, and all owed their loyalty to the new King.

When Solomon was twenty he became King, and held a big service to God at Gibeon. In a dream God asked him to chose a special gift. Remembering how God had helped his father David, he replied: "Oh God, give me wisdom to tell between right and wrong, so that I may rule this great nation with justice."

God was delighted and promised Solomon help, saying he would also give him riches, honour and a long life.

Solomon's wisdom was soon put to the test when two women brought him two babies. One baby was strong and healthy, but the other was dead, and each woman claimed the healthy baby as being hers.

When the King was asked to settle the argument, he told a guard to cut the baby in two, and give half to each of the women.

Solomon knew that the real mother would not let the baby be killed, and when one of the women cried out: "Oh King, don't kill the baby! Rather let this

other woman have it", he knew she must be the baby's mother.

Solomon was a wise young man, and to help him govern, he appointed twelve main officers to be a council with a large number of other leaders under them.

Apart from acting as judges in the various districts, they also had to keep Solomon's great army up to strength.

It was a big task finding supplies for his army. Every day Solomon's palace used thirty containers of flour; sixty containers of coarse meal; thirty oxen; a hundred sheep, and other wild animals and poultry.

While they feasted, Solomon passed on words of wisdom to his friends, and people came from many lands to listen to his three thousand proverbs, and one thousand and five songs.

Solomon built the temple of Jerusalem on Mount Moriah, something his father David had been unable to do because he was a warrior and a man of blood.

Thirty thousand of Solomon's men worked in silence on the building, which was made of stone and cedar-wood.

One Temple court was reserved for the people of Israel, and there was a special courtyard for the priests. A great stone altar, known as the altar of burnt offering, had a large brass basin at the side for washing the offerings.

The real Temple, or Holy Place, was also made of

marble and cedar-wood, and had special rooms for the High Priest and his sons.

The Holy Place was beautifully furnished with a cedar-wood and gold table for the twelve loaves of shew-bread. A heavy curtain stood before the Holy-of-Holies at the back of the Holy Place. Only the High Priest was allowed to enter once a year, on the Day of Atonement.

Inside, the Ark of the Covenant held the two stone tablets containing the Law which God gave Moses on Mount Sinai.

Two pillars, Jachin and Boaz, stood at the entrance to the Temple, which took seven years to build, and stood for nearly four hundred years.

God told Solomon he would always be with him in the Temple, providing he followed in his father's footsteps. But Solomon did not heed God's warning.

The Queen of Sheba brought Solomon camel loads of treasures and saw the splendour of Solomon's courts, and the lovely cedar-wood and gold place called "The House of the Forest of Lebanon". It had walls covered with gold shields and plates. The throne was of ivory and gold and had a lion at each side. Even Solomon's cups were of gold.

To bring all these riches, Solomon had a large merchant navy. His ships brought to the ports in the south of the land, in the Red Sea, great cargoes of gold and precious stones and spices and ivory and peacocks and apes. Those ships must have sailed all

the way to the East Indies, and right down the east coast of Africa. There was no kingdom like Solomon's in all the world.

But all was not well. Solomon was not obeying God's commandments. He had married many wives, and some of them came from heathen nations. He didn't try to teach them to worship the true God, but he let them worship their heathen idols in Jerusalem. He still went himself to the Temple to worship, but he also went with his wives to bow down before idols of wood and stone, and to worship the sun and the moon and the stars. You will remember that God had warned him of what would happen if he turned away to worship false gods. But now Solomon was too rich and powerful even to think about that warning.

Till one day God spoke in judgment to him! This is what God said: "You have not kept my commandments. You worship false gods. Now I am angry with you. Your kingdom will be taken away and given to one of your servants. But because of the faithfulness of your father David, I shall not do this until you die. When this happens, I shall leave only one tribe, the tribe of Judah, to your family, for the sake of David's memory, and for the sake of Jerusalem, the place I have chosen as My own."

From that time on, God allowed troubles to break out in the land of Israel. Edom in the south, and Syria in the north broke away more and more from Solomon's control; and even the people of Israel

were very unhappy about the heavy taxes they had to pay and the unpaid work every tribe had to do on the great buildings in Jerusalem.

God even allowed an opponent to arise for Solomon. He was Jeroboam, the son of Nebat, a young officer in Solomon's army. One day he was travelling along when he met a prophet called Ahijah. The prophet did a strange thing: he snatched off his own new cloak, and tore it into twelve pieces! Ten of the pieces he gave back to Jeroboam, and two he kept. To Jeroboam he said: "That is what God will do. He will break up this kingdom and take it away from Solomon's family. When he dies you will take his place to rule over ten of the tribes. The other two will remain to his family. But you must keep God's Laws and do His Will, or else His wrath will fall on you, too. The wrath of God has come on the family of David, but not for ever."

When the news of this reached Jerusalem, Solomon was furious. He sent out men to kill Jeroboam, but the young man fled to Egypt, and stayed there till the king died. But he had his followers in Israel, and there was much unhappiness there. When Solomon died, the whole great kingdom would break up – and all because the king had become too rich to obey the commandments of God!

JONAH

When Solomon died, the kingdom of Israel split into two. The northern kingdom, which was sometimes called Israel and sometimes Samaria, had ten tribes, but the southern kingdom of Judah had only two. People of both kingdoms had enemies. In the south the Egyptians wanted to rule all the countries round about them, and in the north the cruel Assyrians terrified their enemies, because of the frightful things they did to the people they conquered.

God told Jonah, a prophet who lived in Israel, to go to Nineveh, the capital of Assyria, and warn the people of their great wickedness.

Jonah was afraid and angry at what he had been told to do, and instead of going to Nineveh, he ran away to Joppa, where he found a ship heading for Tarshish on the other side of the Great Sea, where Spain is today.

But Jonah should have remembered that one cannot run away from God, who knew what Jonah was doing.

When the ship was at sea, God created a fierce storm and although the sailors threw everything overboard, it still seemed as if the ship would go down.

When the sailors found that their heathen gods were unable to stop the storm, they went to Jonah who was

asleep below deck, and asked him to call upon his God for help. But the storm grew worse, until the sailors realised that it must be someone on the ship who had caused them to come into such danger. They cast lots to see who it was, and when Jonah told them why he was on the ship, they were terrified that he was trying to escape from God.

When they told him that while he was on the ship they were all in danger of losing their lives, Jonah felt sorry, and asked them to throw him into the sea.

In the end they did what Jonah said, and as soon as they cast him over the side, the wind began to settle, and the waves calmed down.

God sent a great fish to swallow up Jonah, and for three days and three nights while he lay in the stomach of the fish, Jonah prayed to God, and begged for forgiveness.

After the third day God answered, and the fish threw Jonah up on a nearby beach.

Sometime afterwards, God again told Jonah to go to Nineveh and approach the people, but this time Jonah did as he was asked. Nineveh was a very large city, and Jonah walked down its broad streets and into the market places crying out: "Another forty days and Nineveh will be destroyed for her evil."

When they heard Jonah's stern words, and they knew how God had saved him from the stomach of a fish, the people of Nineveh were afraid, and soon even

the king listened to Jonah, and led the people in praying that God would forgive them.

The king was so repentent for his sins that he clothed himself in sackcloth, and sat in ashes to show his sorrow. He called a fast throughout the city, and on the days of fasting, not even the animals were allowed to eat or drink. He also commanded that all the people, and even their animals must be clothed in sackcloth, to show their sorrow for their sins, and the cruelties they had done to others.

Would God spare them, and forgive them, and not destroy their city, as Jonah had said?

But God did see that they were turning from their wrong ways, and were really sorry for the things they had done, and He had mercy on them. He kept back the destruction that was to come on their city.

When the forty days had passed, and Nineveh was still standing, and God had not poured out His anger on the people of the city, Jonah was furious. He could see that the people had changed their ways, he knew all about the great fast that had been held, but that did not matter to him. He wanted Nineveh to be destroyed! He had said that after forty days the city would be smashed to the ground, and now God was not going to do it, and all he had said would seem to be the silly words of a madman!

And Jonah began to sulk. In his prayers, this is what he said to God: "Lord, isn't this what I said would happen, when I was still in my own country? That is

why I fled to Tarshish; because I knew all my work would come to nothing. I knew that Thou art a God of mercy. Who does not easily become wrathful, and that Thou wouldst in Thy kindness forgive their sins. So I felt that it would be really a waste of time for me to come here to Nineveh. But, Lord, it is not worthwhile for me to go on living, seeing I have made such a fool of myself. Take away my life from me, Lord, I pray."

Now, that was a terrible thing to say to God. It was blasphemy, just as if Jonah was telling God He had done wrong in sparing Nineveh. But God was not angry with Jonah; He knew what kind of person His servant was. All He said was: "Is it sensible for you to be angry about this?"

Jonah didn't answer. He flounced out through one of the city gates, and up against the east wall he built himself a shelter of branches. There he waited to see if God would after all punish the city.

It was terribly hot there, and Jonah's shelter of branches didn't protect him very much. But God was watching! He made a gourd, a wild creeper, to grow up over the shelter, and give shade for Jonah. Jonah was very pleased. How much better he felt in the shade cast by the creeper! He did not think, though, about the fact that God had given him the creeper.

But early the next morning God did something else: He sent a worm to gnaw at the stem of the creeper, and in the great heat it soon withered and died. And then, of course, there was no shade for Jonah's head. He

was furious! A hot east wind began to blow, and the sun beat down on Jonah's head, and in his sulky bad temper, he wished he were dead.

Then God spoke to him again: "Are you wise to be angry about the gourd, Jonah?" And Jonah said: "Of course I am! And to be very angry, too!" Then God answered: "Jonah, you are upset and angry about the death of the gourd. You had nothing to do with its growth. I gave it to you, and I took it away, and you are very angry. But this great city of Nineveh, with so many people that there are more than a hundred-and-twenty thousand children, even, in it; you want me to destroy that, and you are angry because I don't. Oh, Jonah, Jonah, won't you think about this again? Surely if you wanted me to spare a gourd, which is nothing, you would want me even more to spare such a great city as Nineveh?"

Isn't that exactly what our Lord Jesus meant when He taught long afterwards: "Love your enemies; bless them that curse you, do good to them that hate you, and pray for them that persecute you?"

We know nothing more about Jonah after this: but the story is kept to remind us that God loves and forgives all who turn to Him, whatever nation they come from.

THE STORY OF DANIEL

When Nebuchadnezzar, king of Babylon, captured Jerusalem, he took Jehoiakim, the king of Judah prisoner, and brought him to Babylon with his family, and some young Israelites.

Nebuchadnezzar, realizing the youths were intelligent and handsome, gave them special food and wine, and had them educated so that they could serve him at court.

Among them was Daniel, whom the king called Belshazzar, and three others, who became known as Shadrach, Meshach and Abed-nego.

Although there was no temple, the four boys were determined to follow God's laws, and serve him faithfully.

The Jews had strict rules about foods, and Daniel knew they should not eat the meat from the king's table, and persuaded the steward to give them vegetable food and water instead.

As the boys gained knowledge, Daniel especially had great understanding of visions and dreams. After three years, Nebuchadnezzar found the boys had became ten times wiser than his own magicians and astrologers.

Time passed and Nebuchadnezzar became troubled

with strange dreams, and ordered all the wise men of Babylon to be killed, because his astrologers and sorcerers were unable to explain a dream which he could not even remember.

When Daniel realized this, he persuaded the king to give him time to explain the dream. That night God showed the secret of the dream to Daniel, who told the king what God had revealed to him.

He told Nebuchadnezzar that he had seen a great image with a head of fine gold; breast and arms of silver; belly and thighs of bronze; legs of iron, and feet of part iron and part clay. As the king had watched, a stone hit the feet of the image breaking them to pieces. The iron, the clay, the bronze, the silwer and the gold all broken to pieces, and were carried away by the wind, until no trace could be found. Then the stone became a great mountain and filled the whole earth.

Then Daniel explained that the head of gold represented king Nebuchadnezzar and that other kingdoms which would follow, would be weak and divided, until one day the God of Heaven could set up a Kingdom which could never be destroyed.

When the king heard this, he fell on his face before Daniel and said: "Truly your God is a God of gods, and a Lord of kings and a revealer of secrets".

He gave Daniel high honour and allowed him to set Shadrach, Meshach and Abed-nego in charge of Babylon.

The three young rulers fell out of favour with the

king, because they refused to worship a golden image, and the king ordered them to be thrown into a raging furnace.

But they told Nebuchadnezzar that their God could save them, and when they walked out of the furnace unharmed, the king praised their God, and decreed that anyone who said anything against Him should be torn limb from limb, and their houses laid in ruins.

Later Nebuchadnezzar's son, King Belshazzar, gave a feast to a thousand of his lords, and ordered that the silver vessels his father had brought from the Temple of Jerusalem should be used for the wine.

As the guests drank, they praised their heathen gods, but as they feasted, they were horrified to see the vision of a man's finger writing on the wall, in a strange language. The king's astrologers and magicians were baffled, but the king sent for Daniel, who warned him against praising heathen gods, and drinking wine from sacred vessels. Then he told the king the words on the wall were: "Mene, Mene, Tekel, Peres.

Mene, God has numbered the days of your kingdom and brought it to an end.

Tekel, You have been weighed in the balances, and found wanting.

Peres, Your Kingdom is divided, and given to the Medes and Persians".

Then the king ordered Daniel to have fine clothes, and be proclaimed third ruler of the land.

That night the Persians swept into the city and

Belshazzar was slain, and Darius the Mede made king. Daniel was highly respected and became one of the three presidents over the hundred and twenty governors of the provinces.

The presidents and governors became jealous of Daniel, and asked the king to establish a law that anyone who prayed to any god, other than the king, for the next thirty days should be cast into the lions' den.

The king was flattered and not realising what he was doing, signed the decree.

But Daniel continued to kneel three times a day to give thanks to God in full view of the people passing his home, and his enemies were quick to tell the king.

Although he tried to find a way of saving Daniel, the king was eventually forced to order Daniel to be thrown to the lions.

Then the unhappy king went to his palace and spent the night fasting; no music was played before him, as usually happened, and he spent a sleepless night.

But in the lions' den Daniel had no fear, and the lions made no attempt to hurt him. He knew why he was safe: God had sent an angel to look after him.

At day-break the king rose up, and hurried to the den of lions, and cried in anguished tones: "Oh Daniel, servant of the living God, has your God, Whom you serve continually, been able to deliver you from the lions?"

And Daniel replied: "Oh King, live for ever! My God

has sent His angel and shut the lions' mouths, and they have not hurt me, because I was found blameless before Him; also against you, Oh King, I have done no wrong."

The king was exceedingly glad and ordered Daniel to be brought out of the den; and it was seen that he was not hurt in any way, because he had trusted in his God.

Then the king commanded that the men who had accused Daniel were to be thrown into the den of lions, and their wives and children with them; and the lions overpowered them, and killed them all. That happened because they hated the servant of the living God, and would not keep God's commandments.

King Darius then wrote to all the peoples, nations and tribes living in all parts of his great empire:

"Peace be multiplied unto you. I make a decree that in every dominion of my kingdom men tremble and fear before the God of Daniel; for He is the living God, enduring for ever; his kingdom shall never be destroyed, and his dominion shall be to the end. He delivers and rescues, He works signs and wonders in heaven, and in earth, He Who has delivered Daniel from the power of the lions."

And so Daniel, who believed and trusted in God, was honoured and respected in all the rest of the reign of Darius the king . . .

THE BABY OF BETHLEHEM

When the story of the New Testament began, Israel was ruled by Herod who had been appointed by the Emperor, Augustus Caesar, of Rome, and Jerusalem was the largest and most important city.

The Jews were tired of being slaves to the Romans and longed for their freedom. They had been told by the prophets that God would send someone to deliver them from their enemies, but they had no idea what He would be like.

At this time there was a young woman called Mary living in Nazareth who was gentle and good, and spent much of her time in prayer.

Mary married Joseph, a poor carpenter who was kind, and hardworking, and everyone respected him.

One day when Mary was sitting alone in her room, she was startled when a voice said: "Do not be afraid, I am Gabriel, the angel of the Lord. I have come to tell you that you are favoured in the sight of God."

The angel told her that she would have a son that she should call Jesus, and that He would be the Son of God, and would reign for ever, and ever.

Mary immediately set out to visit her cousin, Elizabeth, to tell her the joyful news. Elizabeth lived

with her husband Zacharias, about eighty miles away in the city of Hebron in the mountains of South Judea.

Elizabeth told Mary that she too was to have a baby son, who was to be named John, and that the angel Gabriel had told her husband that their son would be filled with the Holy Spirit, and would lead the people of Israel to the Lord.

Mary was overjoyed to hear Elizabeth's news and stayed with her cousin for about three months and they talked of the great happiness that would be theirs when their sons were born.

When Mary returned to Nazareth, the angel Gabriel had already told Joseph about the baby son they were to have, and that He would be the Son of God.

The Roman Emperor, Augustus Caesar, wanted to make a list of all the Jewish people, so that he could collect taxes from them, and Mary and Joseph had to set off on a long journey to Bethlehem to place their names on a special list that would be kept there.

When they arrived in Bethlehem the town was crowded and Joseph was unable to find a room for Mary and her unborn child, but as he was coming away from an inn, the innkeeper, seeing that Mary was exhausted from her long journey, offered them a place in the stable of the inn.

That night Mary's baby boy was born, and she called him Jesus as the angel had said, and laid him a manger filled with sweet-smelling hay.

That night a group of shepherds looking after their sheep in the hills, saw a great light, and in the middle sat an angel of the Lord.

They were afraid and fell down on their knees, but the angel told them not to be afraid because he had come to bring them tidings of great joy. He said that "Unto you and all people is born tonight a Saviour who is Christ the Lord. And this shall be a sign unto you. You shall find the baby wrapped in swaddling clothes, and lying in a manger."

The shepherds set off at once for Bethlehem, and found Mary, Joseph and Jesus in the stable.

After seeing the Holy Child they left Joseph and Mary, and before going back to their sheep, they told everyone what they had seen.

The news spread over the land, but when Herod heard it he was very worried, and when three wise men asked him where they could find "The One who is born King of the Jews," he was even more upset. He gathered the chief priests and learned men together and said: "Where is this child, and who is he?" The chief priests replied: "In Bethlehem of Judea. It was written by the prophets that the Christ would be born there."

Herod was angry when he heard these things, and he said to himself: "Will this baby born in Bethlehem take my throne from me?" So he pretended that he wanted to worship the child, and said to the wise men: "Go and search well for the young child, and when

you have found him, come and tell me, and I will go and worship him too."

As the wise men set out on their journey, a great star shone in the sky, and led them to the place where Jesus lay. When the star stopped over the building where the baby was, they were very glad, and went in to see Him.

There they found Joseph and Mary with the young baby, and they fell at once upon their knees and worshipped Him; and when they opened up their treasures, they put in front of Jesus, gold, frankincense and myrrh – precious gifts to fill the place with beauty, and holy fragrance

After the wise men left the baby Jesus, they did not return to King Herod, as he had told them to do, because while they slept they had a dream telling them not to return. So each of the three wise men returned to his own country.

At the same time an angel of the Lord came to Joseph, and said: "Take the young child, and flee into Egypt. Stay there until I bring word that it is safe to return. Herod is looking for Jesus to kill Him."

So Joseph arose, and prepared the ass, while Mary got everything ready for the long journey. When it was dark, they quietly left the house, and took the road to Egypt.

Not long after they had gone, King Herod's soldiers arrived in Bethlehem, but they did not find the baby, because Joseph had been warned by God.

The journey to Egypt was very hot and tiring, es-

pecially with a young baby. At last they reached the River Nile, and the land of the Pyramids – they had escaped from Herod, and now they were safe.

When they arrived, Joseph and Mary set up their new home in Egypt, and patiently waited for the day when they would be told to return.

About two years later King Herod died, and the angel of the Lord came to Joseph and said: "Take your wife, and Jesus, back to Palestine. It is safe for you to go back."

And so Joseph and Mary packed their things together, and set off happily on the long journey. They did not mind, for they were going back to the land of their birth, to the little town of Nazareth. There Jesus grew into a fine boy, preparing himself each day to serve His Heavenly Father.

CHILD OF NAZARETH

When Jesus was a baby in Bethlehem, three wise men from the east came to visit him bringing gifts.

Although a star had led them to Jesus, they were not sure whether they would find the baby boy, and went to the court of Herod the king to ask whether they could find "The One Who is born King of the Jews?"

Because Herod was afraid that the Baby would one day take away his throne, he called all the chief priests together, and asked them where the Saviour, God had promised, would be born.

They told him that the Holy Scriptures said He would be born in Bethlehem, about five miles away. Herod told this to the wise men, and asked them to let him know when they had found the Child, so that he could also go and worship him.

That night the wise men saw again the star that had guided them. This time it stayed above the very place where Jesus lay. They went into the room where He was, and placed before him gifts of gold, frankincense and myrrh, but that night they did not sleep peacefully, because in a dream an angel warned them not to go back to Herod. The next morning they took a different way back home.

Joseph, Mary's husband, was also warned in a

dream to take Jesus and His mother to Egypt, because Herod the king would try to find the Baby to kill Him.

That night they set off for Egypt, and later they heard that Herod had sent out his soldiers to kill all the boy babies of two years old and under in Bethlehem and the surrounding countryside.

When Herod died, an angel told Joseph to take his family back to their own country. But they didn't go back to Bethlehem, because the angel warned them to go instead to Galilee. Archelaus, another cruel man, had taken the place of his father, Herod, and Joseph settled in Nazareth and took up his work as a carpenter.

Jesus grew up in Nazareth, and despite the lack of the kind of schooling we have nowadays, people were surprised about His great knowledge.

Jesus had a cousin about his age, who later became John the Baptist.

Mary, the mother of Jesus, had a cousin, Elizabeth, who was married to a priest, whose name was Zacharias. Although Elizabeth and Zacharias were old, they both longed for children, and one day an angel from God told Zacharias that they would have a son. When Zacharias heard that they were going to have a baby, he did not believe the news, and was struck dumb. He was unable to speak again until after the boy was born, and was given his name, and presented to God.

Then Zacharias told the people that the baby was to

be called John, and that he would become a prophet of the Most High God.

When John grew up, he became a great preacher and spent much time in the desert praying, and talking to God. All kinds of people came to listen to him preaching and to be baptised by him in the waters of the River Jordan, and one day John had the great privilege of baptising Jesus Christ Himself.

When Jesus was twelve years old, Joseph and Mary, like all other faithful people, went to Jerusalem for the Feast of the Passover, which lasted the whole week.

This was an important occasion, for a Jewish boy at twelve years old could become a "Son of the Law", and could then be treated as a grown-up.

The journey to Jerusalem was long and dangerous because of robbers and bandits, but from the Mount of Olives, just outside Jerusalem, they would be able to see the splendid white marble buildings and the golden roof of the Temple.

At the Passover season there was much business going on in the outer courts of the Temple. On the outside the building was beautiful, but in the court-yard the scene was not so pleasing. There was noise and dirt as traders sold sheep, oxen and pigeons for the sacrifices – and there were money-changers there too, to change the money the people brought into the special Temple. But many of those traders were very dishonest men. The time would come later on when Jesus would drive these people out of the Temple, say-

ing: "Take these things away; you shall not make My Father's house a house of trade."

When the Feast of the Passover had ended, Mary and Joseph joined the party of worshippers from Galilee, and they set off together on the journey home to Nazareth. There was such a crowd that they did not notice that Jesus was not with them, until the end of the first day's journey. Then they went hunting for Him among their relatives and friends, but no one had seen Him. They looked everywhere, but He was not to be found, so they turned back to Jerusalem.

On the third day they arrived back at the Temple, and to their amazement they discovered Jesus sitting in one of the courts among the teachers, listening to them, and asking them questions. A crowd of people had gathered round, and it was easy to see that they were surprised at the young boy's knowledge and the intelligent questions He was asking.

But Mary was upset that her kind and loving son, who had always been so thoughtful, should have worried them so and cried out: "Son, why have you treated us like this? Your father and I have been so worried. We've looked for You everywhere."

"Why did you look for Me?" Jesus answered. "Did you not know that I must be in my Father's house?"

His parents did not understand what He meant by that, but Jesus was telling them that His first work, His great work, would always be to serve God.

From the Temple Jesus went back with Joseph and

His mother, Mary, to Nazareth. There He stayed quietly in the home, as their obedient son, for the next eighteen years, until He had to begin His work of teaching, and in the end to die on the Cross for our sins.

JESUS IN THE TEMPLE

Jesus often visited the Temple in Jerusalem where the Jewish people went to worship God and offered sacrifices for their sins.

It was a beautiful building of white marble and gold. The learned men of the Law came there to argue about God's commandments. Some were godly, but some only wanted to show off their cleverness. In the outer courts were merchants who sold the animals needed for the sacrifices. There were money-changers too, because special money was used in the Temple.

Jesus was twelve when He went to worship in the Temple for the first time. It was the time of the Passover when the Jews remembered how God had brought their forefathers out of Egypt many centuries before.

Jesus travelled to Galilee with His mother Mary, and Joseph, to join in the great Feast, and when it was over Mary and Joseph started back to Nazareth with their friends.

But when they set up camp for the night there was no sign of Jesus. They searched thoroughly, but no-one had seen Him. They went back to the Temple, and found Jesus sitting in one of the courts listening to the teachers, and asking them questions. They were angry

with Jesus, but he answered: "Mother, why did you worry about Me? Didn't you understand that I had to be in My Father's house?"

We know very little about Jesus until he began his work of preaching God's Word and healing the sick. He was often in the Temple worshipping and telling the people how God had wanted them to live, and because he did so, he made many enemies.

One day when he was in the outer court of the Temple, which was crowded with money-changers, and men selling oxen and sheep, the Lord Jesus was disgusted with the noise, and making a whip of thin cords, he drove them all out of the Temple, and overturning the money-changers' tables sending their coins showering onto the floor, said: "This shall be a house of prayer, but you have made it a den of thieves".

When Jesus taught in the Temple, there was always a great crowd to listen to him. Sometimes the scribes and Pharisees listened also, and asked Him cunning questions to try and trap Him.

On one occasion they asked Him if it was right to pay taxes to the Roman Caesar, or not. But Jesus knowing what was in their hearts, asked them to give him one of the coins used for paying taxes.

'Showing them the picture of Caesar's head on the coin, he said to them: "Give to Caesar the things that belong to Caesar, and to God the things that are God's."

At another time he was asked which was the

greatest commandment in the Law. Jesus replied: "You must love the Lord your God with all your heart, and all your soul, and all your mind. This is the first and greatest commandment. The second is like it. You must love your neighbour like yourself. Those two laws sum up all God's commandments."

The Lord Jesus spoke with great authority. He did not argue about things like the rabbis did, so that the listeners were not sure what they meant. When Jesus said a thing, people knew what He meant, and they were sure He was right, too. One day when He was teaching in the Temple, the chief priests sent some soldiers of the guard to arrest Him, and bring Him to them. But when the men came back they were empty-handed. The chief priests were angry. "Why have you not brought Him?" they asked. But they answered: "There never has been a Man yet who spoke like this man. There was authority in all He said, and no one could miss it. But the Pharisees and many of the other learned men hated Him just because He seemed to know all the secrets hidden in their hearts, and they could not answer Him.

One of the things Jesus spoke about most, was the high-and-mighty ways of the Pharisees and the scribes. They claimed to be the only people who really knew anything about God's Law, or kept it properly. But Jesus knew their hearts, and He spoke more stern-ly to them than to any other people. He called them hypocrites, shams; for He said to them: "You steal

away widows' houses, then you go and make long prayers, and you think all is well. Instead, your guilt becomes even greater. You pay tithes to the temple, but you are not worried about the unjust way you treat others, or all your unkindness to people, or even about the promises you keep on breaking. You make a great show of your religion, and walk about like lords among the people. But you have never learned that to become really great you must serve others; or that if you pretend to be great, you will be brought down very low. You serpents, you generation of vipers, how can you escape the punishment of hell?"

Those were the harshest words He ever used, but that is what the Lord Jesus thought of people who pretended to be religious, and made a great show of it, but in their hearts were just selfish.

As Jesus sat in the Temple court one day, he was watching the people who went across to the Temple treasury on the other side. That was where the great boxes were, which held the money people brought as gifts for God's work.

On that day many rich people came to throw their gifts into the boxes – and they made a great show of it too! But as Jesus watched the rich men casting their gifts into the treasure-chests, a poor little widow, very shabbily dressed, quietly slipped in between them, and dropped in her gift. Then the Lord Jesus turned to the people around Him, and said: "Do you see that widow? She has dropped into the treasury only two

mites, the tiniest coins of all we have. But I tell you that she has given more than all the rich men together! What they didn't need for themselves, they have given; but she in her poverty has given everything she had." God knows whether we give to His work because we love Him, and long to see others love Him too; or only because we have to, and want to make ourselves seem important, and good in front of other people.

The Lord taught many important truths in the Temple courts; even some of the parables were told there. Many people gathered there, and so it was a good place to preach God's Word for as many as possible to hear.

But, Jesus warned His listeners that the Temple would not stand for ever. They must not trust in the Temple in all its glory, but in God. Now they boasted of its beauty, and of the clever way its great stones were put together. But Jesus said: "For all their glory now, every single stone in these buildings will be thrown down, and not one building will remain."

For the people who worshipped in the Temple were no longer obeying God.

STORIES JESUS TOLD

When Jesus was about thirty years old, he often preached beside the Sea of Galilee. Sometimes He spoke on the beach, and on other occasions He would stand in a boat to speak to the people from many countries who gathered on the shore.

The stories Jesus told had a special meaning and were called parables.

One parable was about a sower who went out to sow seed. Some dropped by the wayside so that the birds ate them up, or they became trodden into the ground.

Other seeds fell on rocky ground, and the seeds withered away because there was no water to keep them alive. The seeds that dropped on thorny ground became choked by the thornbushes, but the seed that fell on good ground grew into healthy plants, and bore fine fruit because it had been well sown.

Jesus told his disciples they should remember the story, because the seed was the word of God, and the wayside was like the people who heard what God said to them but took no notice. The rocky ground was like the people who listened happily but had no roots as soon as trouble came. The thorny ground was like people who love riches and are always looking for pleasure, but the good soil was like people who were

honest, and remembered God's word and did as He said.

Jesus loved telling people stories and listening to their problems, and He was particularly happy when he was among children. Sometimes his disciples tried to keep them away because they thought He would be disturbed by them, but Jesus always said: "Let the little children come unto me, for they are the people God wants for His kingdom. They are His children."

Another parable Jesus told was of the ungrateful servant who owed a certain king a great sum of money.

One day the king told him that he and his wife and children would be sold as slaves because they could not pay. The king relented when the servant begged for time to pay, but the servant immediately went out, and finding a man who owed him a small sum of money, grabbed him by the throat and threatened to have him thrown into prison unless he paid.

Although the man pleaded for time, the servant refused to listen, and had him sent to prison.

When the king heard this he was very angry and told his servant that he too would have to go to prison until he had repaid all his debt to the king, because of his cruelty.

Jesus told them: "If you do not forgive, neither will God forgive you when you sin against Him."

A parable the people loved to hear was about a good shepherd who had a hundred sheep. When one strayed from the flock he went after it, leaving the

others alone, because every sheep was precious to him.

"This means", said Jesus, "that God will not rest until He has found, and brought home, every one of His children who had wandered away."

Then Jesus would tell them about the parable of "The Prodigal Son."

"A certain rich man," said Jesus, "had two sons, whom he loved very much. One day the younger son came to his father and said: "Please give me my share of the things which you have saved for me, that will one day be mine. I would rather have them now, while I am still young, then I can enjoy myself."

"So the father gave the son his share of his riches, and said no more about it. Not many days after he had done this, the son packed his belongings, and left his father's house.

"The elder brother did not ask his father for his share of the riches. Instead he stayed at home and helped his father to look after his house and land.

"Meanwhile the younger son travelled to a country far away, and settled down amongst strangers.

"At first everything went well for him. He was rich and had many friends. He did not work, but wasted all his money and spent everything that he had on amusing himself. He never stopped to think about his family, who had been so good to him, neither did he bother about anything that mattered in life.

"It was not long before he had spent all his money.

There was nothing left, and his friends deserted him, because he was no longer rich. Then suddenly a famine came upon the land, which meant that there was no food. If he had saved the money, he might have had enough to return to his father, but he was alone and penniless.

"He soon found that he had to look for work, but there was little he was able to do. At last a man offered him a job looking after pigs, which he hated, especially as he was a Jew, to whom pigs are unclean animals, which they must not even touch. But he had no choice, for he was starving. Even with the job, he earned so little, that he still went hungry. He became so unhappy that he began to think how foolish he had been, and he wondered how his family were getting on. While he was so miserable, they had plenty to eat, for their table was always full of good food. There was more than enough for his parents and his brother, and the servants were well fed and cared for too.

"At last the son could bear it no longer, and decided to walk back to his own country. It was very far, and he was tired and hungry. He had only just enough strength left to survive the terrible journey.

"One day when his father was standing outside his house, he saw in the distance a tired, limping man, dressed in rags. Although he was so far off, he at once recognised his son, and ran out to welcome him crying out: 'My son! My son!'

"The tired young man almost collapsed in his

father's arms. He was exhausted and ashamed of what he had done, and said: 'Father, forgive me. I have sinned against God, and no longer deserve to be called your son.'

"But his father brought him into the house, and gave him his robe, put a ring on his finger, and shoes on his feet. 'Bring the fatted calf and let us prepare a great feast,' he said joyfully, 'for my son who was lost is found.'

"At first the elder brother was angry because his father paid so much attention to his worthless brother, but then his father said: 'You have always been a good son to me. All that I have is yours, but we must forgive your brother because he is really sorry. Surely we must rejoice because he has come home.'"

Jesus told many stories like this as he went about preaching to His people. They were very impressed by what He told them, and even to this day we can still learn from the parables that Jesus told to His people – nearly two thousand years ago.

MORE STORIES JESUS TOLD

One of the best known parables is called "The Good Samaritan", which Jesus told when a man asked him what he must do to have everlasting life, and tried to trick Him into giving the wrong answer.

The answer was: "You must love the Lord your God with all your heart and with all your soul and with all your strength and with all your mind; and you must love your neighbour as yourself."

But the man asked: "Who is my neighbour?"

Then Jesus told him about a man on his way from Jerusalem to Jericho who was beaten up by thieves who tore off his clothes and left him half dead by the wayside.

First a priest and then a second man saw him but passed by on the other side.

Presently a Samaritan came along and, seeing, the man poured oil and wine on his wounds and bandaged them and took him to an inn.

The next morning the Samaritan gave the inn-keeper two silver coins and asked him to look after the injured man.

When Jesus asked which of the three men was the

real neighbour, "The man who took pity on him", was the reply.

"Then go and do the same," said Jesus.

Jesus also told the story of the ten maidens who were bridesmaids at a wedding and took lamps with them when they went to meet the bridegroom.

Five were foolish and did not take any spare oil and five were wise and took additional supplies.

When the bridegroom was late, the girls fell asleep, and in the middle of the night when he arrived, the wise girls had oil for their lamps, but the foolish ones had to go and buy some more from a dealer, and when they returned, the bridegroom had already gone in to the wedding feast and the door was tightly shut.

When the foolish girls hammered on the door, the bridegroom answered: "I do not know who you are", and would not let them in.

"What happened to those bridesmaids is what will happen in the Kingdom of Heaven," Jesus told His disciples.

And He told them another story of a man who went abroad on a long journey. He put his servants in charge of his property, giving twelve hundred and fifty pounds to one; five hundred pounds to another, and two hundred and fifty pounds to a third, having first decided who should have the most.

The man with the most money began trading, and made a profit of twelve hundred and fifty pounds. The man who had five hundred pounds made a profit of

five hundred pounds, and the man who had been given two hundred and fifty pounds buried his money in the ground.

When the master came home he praised the two men who had increased their money, but to the third who had been afraid to do anything, he said: "You lazy idler. Take the two hundred and fifty pounds to the man who has two thousand five hundred pounds. For to this man that has, more will be given. But if any man has nothing he will loose even what he has."

Jesus was saying that God expects us to do our best, and not to be lazy and waste our time.

One story Jesus told His disciples was about a king who sent for his servants one day and told them they must pay him all they owed him. One of them was most upset: he owed very much indeed, more than he could possibly pay. And so the king threatened to take all his possessions, and sell him and his wife and children as slaves. How he pleaded with the king! "Give me time, and I will pay you all," he said. The king felt so sorry for him that he forgave him the whole debt. But then the man went out and found one of his fellow-servants who owed him some money. It was only a very small amount, but he took the man by the throat and demanded that he should pay at once. The poor man begged for time, but he would not help him at all, and had him thrown into prison. Now, other servants had seen this, and they went at once to tell the king. When he heard, he was terribly angry. He called the mer-

ciless servant to him, and said: "You wicked man! You begged me to forgive you the very great debt you owed me, and I did. But now you go and refuse to have mercy on your fellow-servant for a very much smaller debt. To prison you go at once, and you stay there in the care of the torturers, till you have paid every penny."

Then the Lord added a very important sentence: "That is how My heavenly Father will treat you too, if you are unwilling to forgive other people from your very hearts."

One day when Jesus was speaking to a crowd of people a man called out: "Teacher, tell my brother to give me my share of the fortune which has been left to us."

"Who made Me a judge over you and your brother?" said Jesus. And He told the brothers: "Be careful of greediness. Life is not really made up of the things you own."

Jesus explained what He meant by telling them another parable. "A certain rich man's land yielded such a wonderful harvest that he thought to himself, 'What shall I do? I haven't enough room to store all my crops. I had better pull down my barns and build larger ones. Then I shall be able to store up all my grain and all my goods. Then I will tell myself: You have enough grain and goods to last for years. Sit back and take it easy. Eat, drink and be merry.' But God said to him, 'Fool! This night your life will be taken from you. Who then will get all you have saved for the

future?'

This is what happens to the man who stores up worldly goods, but does not worry about the riches of God. That is why I tell you not to be anxious about what you are going to eat to keep you alive. Stop worrying about what you are going to wear, for there is more to life than food and clothes. Look at the ravens, they do not sow or reap, neither have they a storehouse or barn. Yet God feeds them. And aren't you much more valuable than the birds? Sell what you own and give it away to charity and get yourself treasures in heaven."

Jesus came to Jerusalem to speak to the people. It was a sad time, for He knew He would not come there again and He had many stern things to say to them. As He arrived at the Temple He stopped to watch the people dropping their alms into the great money-chests. Among the pilgrims and rich merchants, Jesus saw a poor widow trying to slip a coin unnoticed into the chest. Her gift was so small that she hoped no one would see, but Jesus had, and He knew what was in her heart.

As she hurried away He turned to His disciples and said: "Truly I tell you that poor widow has given more than all the others, for she gave all she had."

Jesus spoke a great many wise and wonderful things. Among them were these words: "It is not possible for a good tree to bear bad fruit, or for a rotten tree to bear good fruit. As with trees, so with people. You can tell what they are like by the way they behave . . ."

DISCIPLES OF JESUS

Jesus only taught for three years before His enemies took Him and nailed Him to the Cross, but in those years He chose twelve men He called His disciples, whom He taught to carry on His teaching.

They weren't especially clever men, but they were all men who loved Him – except for one of them, Judas!

Some became great leaders, but others we don't know much about, although all of them had important work to do for the Lord Jesus.

He chose His disciples at several different places. Simon Peter and Andrew were brothers whom He saw fishing in the Sea of Galilee. "Follow Me, and I will make you fishers of men," He told them, and at once they left what they were doing, and followed Him.

Jesus had met the two men before, but it was while He was walking beside the Sea of Galilee that he found two other brothers, James and John, sitting in a boat and mending their nets with their father, Zebedee. When Jesus called them they followed Him at once, leaving their father behind in the boat.

The next day Jesus came across a man called Philip from Bethsaida. When Jesus called him to follow,

Philip wanted to tell his friends, and went off to see a special friend called Nathanael. But Nathanael didn't think it possible for any great teacher to come from a miserable little town like Nazareth. He went off with Philip, however, and was surprised when Jesus greeted him with the words: "Look! a true Israelite, with a heart that is honest through and through."

He was even more surprised when Jesus told him that he had seen Nathanael before Philip had called him, when he was still sitting under a fig-tree.

Nathanael said to Jesus: "Rabbi, Thou art the Son of God, Thou are the King of Israel!" But Jesus told him: "You believe in Me, because I said I saw you sitting under the fig-tree? You will see greater things than this. You will even see the heavens opened, and angels descending and ascending, to and from the Son of Man."

Later, Jesus called other disciples, including Matthew a tax-collector in the city of Capernaum.

It is good to think sometimes of the kind of people they were. James and John loved Jesus, but were impatient that other people didn't listen to what He said.

Once, as they were on their way to Jerusalem, the Samaritans would have nothing to do with them, and would not offer them lodgings for the night, because the Jews and the Samaritans hated one another.

James and John were furious, and asked Jesus to call down fire from heaven upon them, as Elijah had done long ago. Jesus scolded them, however, and said:

"The Son of Man has not come to destroy men's lives, but to save them."

James and John loved Jesus so much that they wanted to be seated at His right hand and His left hand, but Jesus told them that they didn't know what they were asking, and told them sadly: "You will drink from the same cup; but I cannot give you the places of honour in My Kingdom. They will be given to those for whom they are intended by My Father."

Indeed they did afterwards drink from the same cup, and James became the first of the disciples to be martyred, and was put to death by King Herod.

John was a horrified witness at our Lord's death, but afterwards became a great Christian teacher, and was sent in lonely exile to the island of Patmos.

Simon Peter was another disciple whose life was changed by Jesus. His quick tongue sometimes led him into trouble and he didn't know how weak was his own character. Although he knew that Jesus was Christ, the Son of the living God, he didn't really understand what it meant, and when Jesus began to tell His disciples how He must go to Jerusalem and be persecuted by the leaders of the nation, and be killed and rise again from the dead, Peter cried out that it could not happen.

But the Lord said sternly: "Get behind Me, Satan: You do not understand the things of God, but only the things that are of men."

There was another sad occasion too, just before the

Lord Jesus was crucified, when Peter showed how little he understood his own weakness. Jesus was telling the disciples that when the high priest sent soldiers to arrest Him, they would all take fright and run away. Peter was indignant to hear that! He would never run away! Even if all the others fled, he would never! But Jesus said quietly to him: "Peter, this very night, before the cock crows at dawning, you will three times have denied knowing Me." That made Peter angry: it would never happen! But it did. In the early hours of the next morning, while Jesus was being tried in the palace of Caiaphas, the high priest, Peter stood warming himself at a fire in the gateway. And there a servant-girl looked at him and said: "But you are a follower of this Jesus of Nazareth, aren't you?" Three times she asked him, and each time he said angrily that he didn't even know Jesus! But the last time, as he spoke, the cock crowed; and Jesus turned and looked sadly at him, across the courtyard. And Peter rushed out into the darkness, weeping as if his heart would break.

But the Lord Jesus still loved him. After He had risen from the grave, He met Peter beside the Sea of Galilee. There He drew him back in love, a new Peter, a Peter who understood his own weakness, and knew how much he needed Jesus. And to Peter He gave the important work of feeding His sheep, of teaching His people. Jesus can use all kinds of people, if only our lives are changed by Him.

Thomas was the disciple who wanted proof of everything before he would believe; but he was a loving-hearted man after all. After the Lord Jesus had died on the Cross, he was terribly down-hearted. Everything seemed to have come to an end, and Thomas didn't even want to be with the rest of the disciples. And so he missed the wonderful experience they had on the evening of the first Easter Day, when Jesus came and stood amongst them, and talked to them, to show that He was alive, and risen from the dead.

When they met him afterwards and told him, Thomas would not believe. Unless he could put his fingers into the wounds in Jesus' hands, and put his hand into the hole in Jesus' side, he would not believe!

But the next Sunday night, Thomas was with the disciples when Jesus came again. Without asking anything, He turned to Thomas and said: "Thomas, stretch out a finger and feel My hands. Reach out your hand and thrust it into My side; and be not faithless, but believing."

Thomas could only cry out: "My Lord, and my God!"

That was the most wonderful thing any of the disciples said about the Lord Jesus; and that is what all Christians know Him to be: their Lord and their God.

JESUS THE SHEPHERD

Jesus once said to His followers: "I am the good shepherd: the good shepherd gives his life for his sheep. I know all My sheep, and they know Me."

Jesus meant that His people were like sheep, and that He was the shepherd looking after them. Every person mattered to Jesus and that is why He was called the Good Shepherd.

When Jesus went to Galilee he chose twelve men to help Him who became known as His disciples.

They all came from different homes but each of them was ready to give up his life-work to help Jesus.

One day when He was near Capernaum and staying at the home of Simon Peter, He learnt that Simon Peter's mother-in-law was ill with a dangerous fever. Jesus lifted her in His arms, and touched her, and immediately the fever left her, and she became well.

The news of this spread, and soon large crowds gathered outside the door, and people brought their sick for Jesus to heal.

Often Jesus went up into the hills of Galilee to sit among the flowers and trees, where it was quiet, and He could think and pray.

One day when Jesus was in the mountains He saw a boat with his disciples being tossed about in a great

storm. They were unable to row against the great waves, and when Jesus saw their distress, He went quickly to the sea-shore, and walked straight into the rough waters.

When the disciples saw a man walking towards them in the terrible storm, they could not believe their eyes, and they were very frightened, but Jesus called out to them: "It is I, be not afraid!" The moment Jesus stepped into the boat, the winds stopped and the sea became calm. What other man but the true Son of God could have walked on the raging sea and not drowned? This was the second miracle that they had seen in one day.

Earlier the disciples had been with Jesus at a place in the countryside. The whole place was packed with people who wanted to be near Jesus. They wanted to hear His words, and they brought their sick relatives for Him to heal. It seemed that they were gathered around Jesus as a flock gathers around its shepherd.

Even when He had finished preaching to them they would not go away, and Jesus was afraid that they would be hungry, and He said: "We must feed them for there is no place for them to eat here."

The disciples said: "Do You want us to go and buy two hundred pennies worth of bread?"

And Jesus said to them: "How many loaves have we here?"

"Five loaves and two fishes," replied the disciples,

"that is all we can find: they belong to a boy in the crowd."

"Give them to Me," said Jesus, taking the basket of food from the boy. Then to the disciples: "Tell the people to sit down on the grass." Then Jesus took the bread and fish, and lifting it towards Heaven, blessed it. Then, when He broke the bread and the fish and handed it to the disciples, there was so much that there was more than enough to feed the five thousand people sitting around Him. All this came from only five loaves and two small fishes. When the people saw this miracle, they knew that Jesus was sent from heaven, and they believed in Him . . .

Whenever Jesus went into the countryside, children followed Him. They loved to be near Him, and He told them stories, which they loved to hear. Jesus liked to watch the children play games together, and He would laugh as they danced around Him. Sometimes their parents would carry their little brothers and sisters to Jesus, and He would take them in His arms and bless them. No matter how tired Jesus was, He was always happy to have the children at His side . . .

One day Jesus was passing by a certain village, when He heard that there were ten men who had a terrible disease called leprosy. Whoever had this sickness had to stay away from other people, even from their own family. Usually the lepers gathered together in a group outside the town, and kept away from all their friends.

When the lepers saw Jesus coming towards them,

they called out to Him: "Jesus, have mercy on us." He was not afraid of their disease and came up to them saying: "Go to your priests, and by the time you get there you will be cured."

Straight away they went off together and as soon as they came to the priests, found that they were cured just as Jesus had promised.

One day while the disciples were walking along with Jesus, they noticed that He was looking very sad. It was unusual to see Him like this, but at first they said nothing.

As they went along, a rich man who was passing by came up to Jesus and said: "What must I do to live forever in Thy kingdom?" Jesus replied: "You must keep all God's commandments. You mustn't steal or lie. You must always love your parents and help your neighbours."

Then the rich man said: "But I have done all these things. What more can I do?"

"Just one more thing," said Jesus, "will you give up everything that you own and give it to the poor, and then join Me in My work amongst the people?"

The rich man looked ashamed because he knew that although he tried to do all that he could, it was not enough. He liked to be rich, and he was not prepared to give away all that he had. As he went sadly on his way, he felt that he had failed God, yet he couldn't find it in his heart to do anything about it.

Jesus looked sad again, and His disciples said: "What is the matter? You look so sad."

"The time will come soon," sighed Jesus, "when people will turn against Me. They will arrest Me and spit on Me. Then they will take Me away and kill Me."

The disciples looked at one another anxiously, for they didn't understand what Jesus had said. Why should a man be hated who did only good to others?

Yet Jesus knew that there were those who were planning to arrest Him, for they were jealous and afraid of the power which He had. When He thought about these things, He was very unhappy.

When they arrived in the city of Jericho, a great crowd of people had gathered to welcome Him. Near the gate was a poor blind beggar. When he heard that Jesus was near, he cried out with a loud voice: "Jesus, have mercy on me."

As they brought the blind beggar to Jesus, he pleaded: "Lord, let me receive my sight."

Jesus replied: "Your faith in Me has cured you. Receive your sight now." At once the poor beggar could see. He was beside himself with joy as he looked at Jesus, and he praised God with all his heart. When he had given thanks to God, he got up and followed Jesus into the city.

So in this way Jesus went about healing the sick, comforting the sad, and preaching to people who wanted to know more about God. Always He watched over His people as a shepherd looks after his sheep.

HE STILLS THE STORMS

During the three years Jesus went about teaching, He spent much time near the Sea of Galilee, because many of His disciples had been fishermen, and He liked sailing across the Sea from Capernaum with His fishermen friends.

One day He suggested to His disciples that they should sail to the other side of the Sea to the country of the Gadarenes. They made ready a little boat and set off, but before they had gone very far they ran into a violent storm which buffeted about the little boat until it was in danger of sinking.

Jesus was asleep, but the disciples were so frightened they awoke him and said: "Master, do you not care that we are perishing?"

Jesus stood up and scolded the wind, and said to the sea: "Peace, be still!" and at once the wind sank to rest and there was a great calm.

Then He asked the disciples why they had not trusted Him, and when they realised what He had done they were astounded, and asked each other: "What kind of a man is this, that even the wind and the waves obey Him?"

Once after this Jesus sent his disciples across the sea while He went up into the mountain near Galilee to pray. It was getting dark and the waves began to get very rough so that by three o'clock in the morning the disciples were still no more than three and a half miles from the shore.

They were tired and worried that their boat would sink, when they saw a man walking across the water towards them. They thought it was a ghost and cried out in fear. When Jesus called out to them, Peter called back: "Lord, if it be Thou, call me to walk to Thee across the water."

Then as Jesus commanded, Peter bravely set out, but suddenly he remembered the storm, and forgot Jesus, and at once he began to sink.

Immediately the Lord reached out and helped him back to the boat, saying: "Oh, man of little faith, why did you doubt?" As they reached the boat the wind stopped and the waves died down.

Jesus also calmed the storms in people's minds, and when He was in the land of Gadara a poor man who was out of his mind came rushing towards Him and came and worshipped Him. The man lived in caves because he was too dangerous to live with other people in the towns. The people had tried to fasten him with chains, but he was so strong he simply broke them to pieces, and no one was able to calm him.

When Jesus asked the man his name He realised that the man had not one evil spirit, but many. The

spirits pleaded with Jesus not to send them away, but let them go into a herd of nearby pigs.

Jesus agreed; but the pigs rushed down a nearby hillside into a lake and were drowned. The man sat quietly by Jesus and the storm in his mind was over.

In the North of Galilee they brought Jesus a boy who was possessed by an evil spirit. The father was very upset about the boy who had been sick ever since he was a baby.

When he saw the Lord, the poor boy fell on the ground, thrashing around and foaming at the mouth.

Then Jesus said to the father: "Only trust Me. If you will simply believe, even the healing of this boy is possible." Then He ordered the dumb spirit to go out of the boy, and it left his body, crying out and tearing him as it went. The boy lay still and many who were watching said: "He is dead!" But Jesus took him by the hand and lifted him up; and he stood up, well in body and mind, and went home with his father, while everyone rejoiced.

Sometimes the storms in people's hearts did not come in the terrible ways we have been hearing about. They often came because the devil had tempted people into doing wrong things until they had the name of being bad persons. Then if they were sad about it, they would keep to themselves, mourning about what they had become. Or else they became defiant, and just kept on doing bad things to spite everyone else. I'm sure you will understand how people can get like that.

But when anyone who was like that came to the Lord Jesus, He understood how troubled they were in their hearts. One of them was Mary of Magdala, who had been a great sinner; but Jesus drove away the evil spirits who led her into doing wrong, and she became one of His most faithful disciples. Do you know how she showed her gratitude? One night when Jesus was resting with His very dear friends, Martha and Mary and Lazarus in Bethany, as He lay beside the low table for the evening meal, Mary Magdalene came into the room. In her hands she had an alabaster jar of very expensive perfumed ointment. She poured the ointment out on Jesus' hair and some on His feet as well; and she even wiped His feet with her own hair! The whole house was filled with the scent of the ointment. Now, some of the disciples were very annoyed about it, they thought that to pour out valuable ointment like that was very wasteful. One of them, Judas Iscariot – the same man who later betrayed Jesus to the high priest – complained and said: "Why wasn't the ointment sold, and the money given to the poor?"

But Jesus said to him: "Leave her alone. She has done for Me what she could, to show her gratitude and love. The poor are always with you. You will have many chances to help them; but I shall not be here always. I tell you, Judas, that from now on, wherever this gospel is preached, people will remember what this woman has done, and honour her memory."

Then there was little Zacchaeus, who lived in

Jericho. He was a tax-collector, and not a very honest man, either; but when Jesus came to the town, and he found he couldn't see Him through the crowd because he was so short, he climbed up into the branches of a tree. And there Jesus found him and called him down because He wanted to eat in Zacchaeus' home that night. The little man was overjoyed; but the people grumbled. How could Jesus go to eat in the home of such a crooked man? But they did not understand what Jesus did: how troubled Zacchaeus was in his heart about the things he had been doing!

And then Zacchaeus said in front of them all: "Lord, I will give half of my goods to the poor; and if I have taken anything away from a person dishonestly, I will give back four times as much." The Lord said to him: "This day salvation has come to your house."

Even being with Jesus, clears the storms out of a person's heart and mind. The same Jesus who stilled the storms on Galilee, can still the storms in our lives, even today.

JESUS, FRIEND OF THE NEEDY

Jesus loved little children and enjoyed talking to them, but one day when a group of mothers brought their little ones to see Jesus and be blessed by Him, his disciples thought Jesus was too tired and told the mothers to take them home.

But Jesus was cross and said: "Suffer little children to come unto Me and forbid them not . . . Let the little children come to Me; do not stop them . . . for such is the Kingdom of God."

Jesus was telling the disciples that God wanted trusting people in His Kingdom, like little children. As he went from village to village the crowds followed him and he taught them that God was THEIR Father. That he loved them and they should love Him in their hearts.

He healed the sick and worked many miracles, and the people went away and told their friends what they had heard and seen.

Because Jesus knew He had little time in which to complete His work He went up onto a mountainside to ask God's help in choosing twelve special disciples to help Him.

He trained these disciples to carry on His work

when He was gone and later gave them power to heal and cast out unclean spirits. Then He sent them, two at a time, to go out to preach and heal.

One day when Jesus had healed a sick child suffering from fits, by laying His hands upon the child and blessing him, His disciples asked why they had been unable to cure the boy. Jesus replied that it was because they had so little faith.

Jesus loved telling stories known as parables, and one day Jesus was going with Jairus, a ruler of the synagogue, to see his daughter who was dying, when a sick woman who had been ill for twelve years, reached out of the crowd and touched His cloak.

At once a wonderful feeling ran through her body and she was cured, but Jesus felt some of His power leave him and said: "Who touched Me?" The woman was frightened, but Jesus smiled and said: "Daughter, your faith has made you well. Go in Peace."

Just then a messenger told Jairus that his daughter was dead, but Jesus told him: "Do not fear, only believe." He sent everyone away but His disciples Peter, James and John, and when he saw everyone in the house was weeping and wailing he said: "Why cry? The child is not dead but sleeping." When the mourners laughed he turned them out of the house. Then he took the twelve year old girl by the hand and said: "Get up little girl", and she got up and walked.

Jesus did many miracles, and one day at Capernaum the crowds were so large, many had to stay outside the

house where He was preaching, and four men carrying a man who was paralysed could not get in. They lowered the man on a mattress through a hole in the roof. Jesus looked up and realising their faith said to the helpless man: "My son, your sins are forgiven."

This did not please some of the people who thought that Jesus was saying what only God had any right to say. "Only God can forgive sins," they thought. Although they did not say the words out loud, Jesus knew what they were thinking and asked them why they thought this. "Which is easier to say?" He asked. " 'your sins are forgiven', or to say: 'Rise, take up your bed and walk'?"

The doubters did not answer and Jesus went on: "But so that you may know that the Son of man has power on earth to forgive sins;" then he turned to the sick man and said gently: "I say to you, rise, take up your bed and go home."

The young man at once got up from the bed and stood up straight and tall. The people were amazed as he rolled up his bed and hurried away to meet his friends. There was gladness and rejoicing, and the people praised God and said to one another: "We have never seen anything like this."

As time went on, more and more people in Judea and Galilee followed Jesus and believed in Him. Now He had seventy more disciples He could trust and send out to preach to the people and help the sick and suffering. The first twelve were Jesus' special helpers,

His Apostles. who went about with Him from place to place.

Their names were Peter, or Simon Peter, Andrew, James and John, Bartholomew, sometimes called Nathanael, Philip, Thomas, Matthew, James the Less, Thaddaeus, Simon the Canaanite and Judas Iscariot.

Some of the disciples wrote down the things that Jesus said and did. That is how we know about His life on earth, the miracles He did, the way He lived and worked.

One day when Jesus had finished praying, one of His disciples said to Him: "Lord, teach us to pray."
And Jesus said to them: "When you pray, say:
    'Our Father, which art in heaven,
    Hallowed be thy name.
    Thy kingdom come.
    Thy will be done on earth,
    As it is in Heaven,
    Give us this day our daily bread,
    And forgive us our trespasses,
    As we forgive them that trespass against us.
    And lead us not into temptation,
    But deliver us from evil.
    For thine is the kingdom, the power and the glory
    For ever and ever, Amen.'"

Another day the disciples came to Jesus saying: "Who is the greatest in the Kingdom of Heaven?" And Jesus called a little child to Him and put him in

the midst of the disciples and said: "Truly, I say to you, unless you change and become like children, you will never enter the Kingdom of Heaven. Whoever humbles himself like this child, he is the greatest in the Kingdom of Heaven."

When the time came for Jesus to go to Jerusalem He took His twelve disciples with Him. They were joined by a great crowd of men, women and children who were going to worship in the Temple. Two blind men were sitting by the roadside and when they heard that Jesus was passing by they cried out: "Have mercy on us, Son of David."

The crowd scolded them, telling them to be silent, but they cried out again: "Lord, have mercy on us, Thou Son of David." Jesus stopped and called them saying: "What do you want Me to do for you?"

"Lord, let our eyes be opened," cried the poor men. Jesus' heart was filled with pity and He touched their eyes and instantly they could see; and they joined the followers.

When they came near to the city, Jesus sent two of His disciples into a nearby village to fetch an ass and a colt. When the people saw Jesus riding into the city on a donkey, they spread their cloaks on the ground for Him to ride over, and cut branches from palm-trees and spread them on the road.

Little children were there too, and all the people shouted out together: "Blessed is He who comes in the name of the Lord. Hosanna in the highest!"